5 BREAK-FREE TRUTHS

Break free of Your Cage and Reach Your Potential

I0223849

VIJAYA SUVARNA
AMOL MULEY

JAICO PUBLISHING HOUSE

Ahmedabad Bangalore Bhopal Bhubaneswar Chennai
Delhi Hyderabad Kolkata Lucknow Mumbai

Published by Jaico Publishing House
A-2 Jash Chambers, 7-A Sir Phirozshah Mehta Road
Fort, Mumbai - 400 001
jaicopub@jaicobooks.com
www.jaicobooks.com

5 BREAK-FREE TRUTHS
ISBN 978-93-86348-48-7

First Jaico Impression: 2017

5 BREAK-FREE TRUTHS

Contents

	Introduction	1
1	Your Truth 1	13
2	Your Truth 2	49
3	Your Truth 3	77
4	Your Truth 4	117
5	Your Truth 5	145
6	Your Truth 6	189
7	Case Studies of Discovering 'The' Truth	203
	Acknowledgements	215
	About the Authors	220
	About Liberation Group	222

Introduction

'YOUR' TRUTH V/S 'THE' TRUTH

There are two kinds of truths in this world – 'Your' Truth and 'The' Truth. And 'Your' Truth is what is stopping you from achieving extraordinary success.

According to Merriam Webster, the simple definition of *truth* is

- the real facts about something: the things that are true
- the quality or state of being true
- a statement or idea that is true or accepted as true

At a basic level, we all want to tell 'the truth'. Why would anyone want to lie if there was a choice? Truth, at least in theory, is simple, straight, clean and clear. Truth does not have a scandalous past that can be dug up in the future. Truth does not have a nefarious history that can rise up from the grave to haunt us. Truth is always easy to manage, because the one who tells the truth is always liberated.

Like we were saying, all that sounds simply lovely… in theory.

But 'simply lovely' is boring. As human beings, we are always fascinated by the complex. We love zigzags and mazes. We like imagery, mystery and intrigue. We love the unconventional. We pride ourselves on our imagination. An experience, unless embellished with gems of extensions and exaggerations, is hardly worth listening to.

And most importantly, we do not have the patience or the courage to untangle a situation and come clean with the absolute truth.

So, we spin a web of lies on a daily basis whenever we feel unprepared to face the truth. And these untruths and half-truths are justified (so we tell ourselves) because it is always to save something or someone, right?

Some typical situations which compel us to lie are –

You have just been invited for dinner and drinks by your client, a lady. And your wife is waiting for you to come home and take her out to dinner. Why would any sane-headed man say that he is going out for cocktails and dinner with a lady client? A simple lie – "I have to stay back at the office, sweetheart. There is a very important tender that I have to submit" – can save your wife's feelings, the day (in fact, the next several days) and most importantly, your head.

· · ·

Your 4-year-old son has been watching very keenly as you sip one martini after another at a party. He walks up to you and says, "What are you drinking? Can I also have a sip?" A simple lie – "This is medicine, sweetheart. The doctor has prescribed this for me. Let us get you a soft drink instead" – can save you a long, complicated explanation.

· · ·

Your oldest client has a brat of a son, who is rude, arrogant, uncouth, selfish and extremely incompetent. Unfortunately, he is also the apple of his father's eye, and the poor man can see no wrong in his foreign-returned, MBA qualified heir. He has handed over the reins of his business to him and is consulting him for all kinds of important decisions. In a rare moment of emotion, your client asks you, "I am really proud of my son and I am sure that he will take my business to heights that I never dreamed of. What do you think?" Now a small lie – "I think he has good potential and I am sure that under your guidance he will touch the heights of success" –

will not only make your client a happy man, but will result in more business for you.

• • •

Your colleague and friend has just nominated himself for "The Leader of the Year" award in your organization. It takes you all your effort not to burst out laughing at his pompousness. The number of people who have left from his department in a year cannot be counted on your fingers and toes together. He is self-centred, incompetent and a very poor people manager. And to your surprise (read 'disgust') he has actually been shortlisted. You are now being asked to give your feedback and comments on his nomination... in front of him. And there he is looking at you eagerly, grinning from ear to ear. Just a small lie here – "He is an enthusiastic worker, a dedicated leader and a good team player. Definitely worth considering" – will ensure that your working relationship with him remains unhampered.

• • •

Your fiancé is looking terrible in her new haircut. (You never liked women with short hair anyway) She is eagerly tossing her head and hair this way and that to elicit songs of praise from you. A small lie – "You look very different. That's a smart new look, honey" – can save your relationship (remember, she is not yet married to you). And anyway hair will always grow back... hopefully!

• • •

You got the gist. These are small lies that help you save face, keep you from embarrassment, make people feel good about themselves, stop an argument from turning into a fight. These small lies hurt no one, but rather help in cementing relationships. These lies are sweet. These lies are innocent. These lies are forgivable.

But what is not forgivable is the other kind of lies – lies that we tell ourselves day in and day out. Lies that are designed by us as defence mechanisms against the world and the people in our circle of influence. Lies that hide our incompetence. Lies that are a cover for our falsehood, our hypocrisy. Lies that don't allow us to see our potential. Lies that don't allow us to experiment, to explore, to experience. Lies that alienate us from people who really matter. Lies that make us live a life that is ordinary and mediocre; when the truth could have made us reach the highest pinnacles of success.

This book is about these bigger, more serious lies that you tell yourself every day. These lies are repeated so often that you now believe them to be the truth. These lies are so devious that they are never discovered for a long time, sometimes even after you are no more in this world.

Let me tell you something. You have a choice of putting down this book right now. Because once you start reading, there is no point of return.

You will see your mirror image in the lies as they unfold one layer at a time. Then when the truth is revealed, the experience will be painful. You will frown when you see yourself as the villain in this book and eventually, you will smile when you recognize that you are the hero too. Each story, each dialogue, each parable, will touch you at the core of your being. Because this book is about YOU and the five Break Free Truths that will set YOU free.

So going back to definitions of truth, you know we are talking about "a statement or idea that is true or accepted as true".

OUR TRYST WITH 'THE' TRUTH

Being corporate trainers, business coaches and OD (Organization Development) consultants has been rewarding for us in more ways than one. Our training, coaching and consultancy interventions across the nation give us the opportunity to meet hundreds of new faces every day – corporate professionals, SME employees, government officials, police officers, school and college students, business owners, managing directors and CEOs, political leaders, working women and even homemakers. You name them, we have trained them.

Some of them are highly successful, some are struggling hard to be, while many others haven't yet begun their journey. Our interactions with them always leave us awed with the lifelong psychological impact of ordinary phrases and daily conversations. Thus we have a huge collection of the most commonly held beliefs (read "their" truths) of people. (In case you wondering, we have documented evidence of this in our thousands of pages of minutes and conversation transcripts – confidential of course. Quite an eye-opener that). These beliefs are generally repeated again and again in the form of platitudes till it becomes the ruling truth of their lives.

As you progress through this chapter, you will find many of your beliefs echoed by others. So, at least you can feel reassured about the fact that you are not alone in this painful journey of self-realization.

However, whether your belief is 'your' truth or 'the' truth depends upon whether it passes the Liberation Coaches' 4-Way Truth Test discussed later in this chapter. Relax! It is a test, not an examination.

MOST COMMONLY HELD BELIEFS

We are sure you already know that our beliefs are a product of our past experiences and upbringing. These beliefs are passed on to us by our parents, siblings, relatives, teachers, uncles, aunts and other people in our circle of influence, including celebrities and our role models.

Certain beliefs pertain to us as individuals ("I was born unlucky" or "I will never be able to score full marks in maths"), while others are concerned with the world around us ("All dark people are dirty" or "The world is filled with bad people").

Thus there can be two categories of beliefs –

1. Beliefs that have *us* at the centre and
2. Beliefs that have other factors at the centre.

All of us tend to have these two beliefs in different proportions and combinations.

Beliefs that have Us at the Centre

People with beliefs having themselves at the centre are said to have an Internal Locus of Control. Such people attribute their successes or failures to reasons within… like their own competence, their utilization of resources, their own drive, etc.

You might think that is great, isn't it? But, people with a strong Internal Locus of Control are found to be self-confident, self-motivated and possessing a high degree of achievement motivation, *only* when the beliefs are 'Truths'. On the other hand, if people with strong Internal Locus of Control hold on to several 'Untruths' as their beliefs, they tend to feel ashamed and guilty most of the time.

	Belief	*Resultant Emotion*
Untruth	I know nothing about this job, I am bound to be a failure	Shame / Guilt
The Truth	I know nothing about this job, but I am willing to learn and become successful	Confidence / Motivation

We meet hundreds of people who have Untruths supporting their Internal Locus of Control. These are the people who feel that they have been working all the time but haven't made any real progress in their lives or careers. There are several others who are quite often put to shame by their monthly or annual reports. Several professionals confess to us in private that many times they don't work as hard as they should, but get away with it because there's nobody to question them.

Jignesh is a Sales Manager with one of our clients. This is what he shared during one of the performance reviews that we conducted– "There are times when I don't feel like pushing myself. These are especially the times after I have lost a deal or I have faced strong-arm tactics from any of my customers. Then... I avoid phone calls from clients. I sit at my desk going through proposals and enquiries for hours. I pretend to 'be at work'. When people ask why I didn't respond or why things got delayed, I often get away by saying 'I was busy'. Who is going to cross-check anyway? I know that my capacity is 100 times more than this. While I can put in 16 hours of active work a day (which I have done in the past), I end up working for only four hours. Well, who is there to question me?"?

Many students and professionals, definitely agree that there were many days, many months, in which they could have worked harder... but didn't. People share how they keep setting goals every year "but don't quite achieve it. There were too many personal challenges!"

A Vice-President of Operations of one of our corporate clients remarked recently – "I have been demotivated for quite a long time now and I am tired of being that way." A successful business-owner, who is part of our Executive Coaching Program made a very realistic observation about himself – "It is difficult to break my laziness habit. I know that it is a definite career hazard, yet I find it difficult to overcome. There's too much gap between the kind of energy that I should bring and what I actually bring to the table. Others may not know this, but I know that I am lazy."

In the above cases, just because they have high Internal Locus of Control, does not necessarily mean that they are living an empowered life. The kind of deeply ingrained beliefs ('Their' Truths) that they have about themselves stops them from realizing their true potential because for them *their* belief is *The* Truth.

Beliefs that have Other Factors at the Centre

On the other hand, people focusing outward are said to have External Locus of Control. Such people attribute their successes and failures to other people and worldly conditions.

When their beliefs are 'Truths', they tend to be cooperative and caring. Such people make good team-players and leaders because of their ability to trust others and make the most of any situations. But when their beliefs are 'Untruths', they become suspicious and insecure of others. Such people tend be quite aggressive and generally find working with others difficult.

	Belief	*Resultant Emotion*
Untruth	My team members are quite politically motivated, they would rather see me fail.	Aggression / Insecurity
The Truth	My team members are quite trustworthy, they point out my weaknesses because they want me to succeed.	Trust / Care / Cooperation

While on one hand, there is a sizeable population that finds faults within themselves, there is the other half that is generally unhappy with the world or the conditions therein. These are the ones who have External Locus of Control.

"I always end up working alone," comments Rafique, who is a project manager with a project management consulting firm of repute. "Our organization is full of sycophants and critics. There is no third category," he says. "Every time I take up a new task or assignment that might improve the efficiency of our project, I am met with tremendous resistance from my own team."

This experience was shared by Mr. Narendra Shah during one of our courses for business-owners. Mr. Shah was finding it more and more difficult to cope up with the needs of his growing business because of his formidable temper. His inability to manage his anger has led to employee retention issues, strained relationships with vendors and lost opportunities from customers. "When I get angry, I just can't focus. I've been this way since childhood. You see, I had a tough childhood. We stayed in a very ordinary locality, our parents were trying to make ends meet and resources were scarce. So, tempers would flare every now and then. That temper is ingrained quite deep in me."

A senior police officer of a State Police Force commented in one of our Training of Trainers Program, "I had so many dreams when I joined the force, they have all died their natural death in the 'system', today I only wait for the day to get over so that I can just go home and forget about my dreams."

Several other business-owners and professionals tell us that they were pretty excited at one time regarding their business and career, that they were passionate at one time. But, after several years of facing *reality*, all that passion seems to be lost somewhere.

This External Locus of Control has made them believe that nothing is in their control. They believe that the world is at fault and it is because of this that they are the way they are.

You will find several more examples of real people in the last section who have had the courage to face their deepest beliefs. their Truths and converted them into avenues for living The Truth.

THE LIBERATION COACHES' 4-WAY TRUTH TEST

While you read through this book, you will come across several beliefs that others have shared with us. You will find some of your own beliefs mirrored in these. But, don't stop at merely identifying with them and saying, 'Yes, that's me! I have said that before!' Take the next step of identifying whether these are 'Your' Truths or 'The' Truths using the Liberation Coaches' 4-Way Truth Test.

Ask these questions every time you are confronted with a belief.

Q.	Question	Yes/No
1	Does 'My' Truth reflect positively on me?	
2	Does 'My' Truth reflect positively on others?	
3	Do I have an evidence to prove that my belief is 'The' Truth?	
4	Does holding on to my truth make me feel empowered and in charge of the situation?	

As a simple rule, if all the four Tests are not answered with a resounding 'YES', we can fairly assume that 'Your' Truth is not 'The' Truth or is only partially representing the truth. Mind you...not just one or two 'YES's. For your truth to be qualified as 'The' Truth ALL the four Test Questions must be answered in the affirmative.

HOW TO USE THIS BOOK

Read one Truth at a time. It is not a novel which you must run through and finish in one single sitting. It is not fast food. It is like a delicacy that needs to be savoured. Imagine having a very small portion of your favourite sweet. Would you gulp it down? Definitely not. You would eat it one tiny bit at a time so that it lasts longer and you can savor every bit, right? This book is to be enjoyed the same way.

While reading this book, let your brain do some thinking. Retrospect, introspect, dig in and wonder whenever a sentence or an idea or a story awakens something within you. Ask yourself tough questions while the truth unravels. Let your mind work and plan to find how each truth can be made a part of your daily routine. Find opportunities to apply the truths. Check if opportunities have slipped away during the day and how you will leverage them tomorrow.

Thirdly, don't just think, *act*. Convert your thoughts into action. If you see that you have been lying to yourself, take a proactive step to ensure that you do not repeat it. Make charts, posters, post-its, stickers... whatever it takes to remind you constantly of your decision to face the truth. Work on it as though facing up to the truths were your life's mission, which in a way it is.

Share. Share your thoughts, your feelings, your realizations, your awareness, your decisions. Find someone you really connect to – *your truth partner*. Don't forget to gift them a copy of this book as you enlist them to help you face up to the truths. Sharing is easier when the other person is undergoing the same process of self-discovery that you are. Slot in a time, perhaps once a week for the next six weeks with that person. The single agenda of this meeting being sharing the journey of discovering your Five Break Free Truths with each other. Remember, the more the Truth Partners, the stronger the motivation.

Spread the Truth! When you have three people as your 'Truth Partners', form the 'Truth Group'. The 'Truth Groups' are teams of four who understand each other and are on the journey to self-transformation. Several 'Truth Groups' together will form the 'Truth Community'. The 'Truth Community' is a community of forward-looking people who are in search of the truths, who are willing to challenge 'their truths' and who are willing to work with other 'Truth Groups' in their endeavour to create a 'Truthful Society'.

Think of this book as a six week journey. This journey has to be repeated several times in a year. Read this book till your mind is programmed into rejecting Your Truths and accepting The Truths. There is THE 5 BREAK FREE TRUTHS TRACKER after every section to help you plan your reading and implementation. Send us a mail once you finish your journey. Tell us your discoveries about yourself. Share with us your successes. Let us weave your experience into another beautiful story for our millions of readers.

And finally, once you have finished this book, mail us your details on learningtools@liberationcoaches.com and we, in turn, will mail you a beautiful certificate that can be downloaded and displayed. The certificate is evidence that you are someone who has the courage to face up to self-limiting perceptions and lies. We will also add your name to the BFT (Break Free Truthsters) Club and you will be entitled to special offers and discounts on all our audio/video products, publications, seminars and consultancy services.

1

Your Truth

1

I am like this because of my circumstances

I could have achieved more if it had not been for others...
My wife simply does not cooperate with my ideas...
I was born in a very poor family. So, I never had ANY advantages...
My boss is very unhelpful. How do you expect me to....
I don't have anyone who helps me...
My entire family is uncooperative. So I can't achieve anything...
People – my colleagues, my friends, my relatives... they always try
*   to demotivate me...*
Our very culture is like that of crabs. They always pull down the one
*   who tries to get on top...*
Do you even know the environment in which I was brought up?
I could have done so much, if only I had had a godfather...
I have no one around to support me...

If the above is the story of your life, welcome to the 'I-am-like-this-because-of-my-circumstances' club. There are millions of members in this Club. You might have come across several of them. And to tell the truth, you might be an active member (unconsciously, I am sure) for several years now. Perhaps, you became a member when your first opportunity was handed over to someone else who didn't deserve it (Or at least, that's what you still believe).

When a person is a member of this club, he finds a lot of company. There are many who have a grouch against the world. They are convinced that the entire world is in a conspiracy against them. They are sure that if circumstances had been different they would have been Amitabh Bachchan, Shah Rukh Khan, Aamir Khan and Salman Khan all rolled in one. "If only... then I would have...." is what gives them their daily dose of sad tragic sighs and conversation starters.

Are you one of them?

What's Your Story?

Below this paragraph, you will find a table that is designed to enable you to face Your Truth.

Step 1

The Belief – Pick out one or similar sentences from the previous page that you have been uttering or thinking regularly.

Step 2

The Evidence – Write down at least one instance when those sentences have been repeated by you so often.

Step 3

The Outcome – Write your feelings when you have 'proved' that the sentences are your life's 'Truth'.

The Belief ……..	The Evidence ……..

The Outcome ………

Step 4
Read on…

THE STORY OF TWO BROTHERS

Not so long time ago, there lived two brothers, Mahesh and Suresh. Mahesh was 11 and Suresh was nine. They lived in a small rundown locality of a big city with their parents. Mahesh and Suresh were extremely poor and led a hand-to-mouth existence. They rarely had a full meal and their clothes were threadbare. But I guess, their life was no different from the hundreds of others who lived in the same city. We all know of poor children who barely have any food to eat but yet have more than enough of laughter and love. How many times have we envied the carefree games and giggles of children who run half-naked around the streets while their parents beg for a living. And you bet there are still thousands of others whose daily hunger is only satiated because they have the arms of their parents around them.

But Mahesh and Suresh were not among these "fortunate" children. Their life was poor, not only because of the lack of food or clothes or books. Their life was all the made poorer because they had a beastly father. Their father was a cruel man. He was an alcoholic, a gambler and a womanizer. He was uneducated, and a wife and child beater. Every day Mahesh and Suresh would hide under the bed and sob as they heard the screams and moans of their mother and watched her get beaten up by their father. The beatings would continue till he collapsed on the bed drunk and slobbering or until their mother lost consciousness. They were terrified of him and had already faced his wrath several times in the past when they had tried to intervene. They only wished they knew why he hated them all so much, because they yearned for his love.

The mother, a gentle and loving soul, had long ago banished any ray of hope for a better life. Her tattered clothes barely managed to cover her battered and bruised skeletal frame.

It hadn't been always like this. She had been a pretty, soft-spoken, cheerful, village belle who had been swayed by the prospect of marrying a man from the city. She had been unaware that beneath the rugged looks, there lurked a man who was an animal. She happily came to the city after her marriage, believing all the stories of 'and they lived happily ever after' that she had heard and seen in movies. Little had she known that she was entering a life of hell. The reality of living with a man who was as barbaric as her husband, shocked her into submissiveness. She had truly believed that if she tried hard enough, if she loved hard enough, if she prayed hard enough, she could change her husband. But what changed was the degree of brutality, which escalated year on year.

Over the years, the pretty girl was transformed into a nervous wreck of a woman who was terrified of her husband, his temper, his demands and his beatings.

Knowing that if she did not bring in any income they would starve to death, she worked as a domestic help in a few houses nearby and managed to keep body and soul together for her little boys, whom she loved with her life. Though there was never enough to eat, she would willingly sacrifice her morsels so that her sons had a little more on their plate. And though she was constantly sick because of the lack of food, rest and peace, she faced her circumstances bravely, without complaining, all her hopes of a better future were pinned on her children.

You know what happens to people who drink too much. They die sooner than expected. And that's exactly what happened to Mahesh and Suresh's father. One day, he suddenly died. He was weaving his way back home, a bottle in his hand. He stumbled, crashed his head against a rock in his drunken stupor and was too comatose to even realize when the life ebbed out of his wasted body. You must be thinking, 'What a relief. Now at least the woman could live in peace with her children.' For a couple of months, they did. But the years of torture had taken its toll. It was almost as though the mother had been alive just to save Mahesh and Suresh from the beatings of their father. She fell seriously ill and never recovered. She passed away in her sleep. The kind-hearted neighbors did what they could for a few days. Served them food and helped them to overcome their grief. But kindness cannot compensate for lack of resources. So even though they wished to, they couldn't continue providing for the two little boys.

And both Mahesh and Suresh, having nowhere else to go, found themselves admitted to an orphanage with just a meager bundle of rags to show as their worldly possessions.

You might be aware that all orphanages have an age limit of 18 for their wards. By then, the children are usually given their basic education and some vocational training. Based on the availability of jobs, which are scarce, and the active involvement of NGOs, these young boys and girls are then placed with organizations for doing mundane work. It is assumed that this is adequate preparation for them to survive independently in the real world.

Mahesh was the first to leave the orphanage. He found a job as an office boy in a small organization. His salary was paltry and his work tough. But that didn't deter him from joining night college and continuing his education. But he realized within a month that he had no money left even for basic necessities, leave alone books and uniform. So, he took up a part time overnight job as a store keeper in a warehouse.

He started his day at the office at 08.30 am and would work till 8.30 pm. He would then gulp down some dinner, reach night college at 09.30 pm and attend classes till 11. Then he would rush to his overnight job. He needed the additional income to support his education, buy second hand books and decent clothes. He would reach home at 4.30 am in the morning. Quickly nap for a couple of hours and then be the first to reach office at 08.30 am, as cheerful and as excited as someone who has had his ten hours of beauty sleep.

Over the next five years, he completed his graduation and got promoted as a Sales Officer. Always used to hard work, he became a top salesperson in no time. Seeing that the new breed of Sales Executives were far more equipped and competent to close larger deals, he started attending seminars and training programs and absorbed not just the topic but also the nuances of behavior and language from the successful people around him. Not satisfied with random education and knowing that in order to progress, one needed to upgrade one's knowledge as well as skills, Mahesh enrolled for a part-time MBA Program and went on to do his Ph.D. He was a voracious reader and had a mega appetite for innovation, ideas and knowledge.

Simultaneously, he kept growing in the organizational hierarchy. His good humor, hard work, commitment and humility made him a great team mate and eventually an inspiring leader. And no one was surprised, when at the age of 40, he became the youngest CEO of the company and led his team to bag the Fastest Growing Company Award at the National Industry Growth Awards within three years.

Knowing that Mahesh had begun his life in a slum and then at an orphanage, a proactive journalist decided to write an article on Mahesh's success. The rags-to-riches story was always a hit with the readers. But before meeting Mahesh, he decided to do some background research.

YOUR TRUTH 1 21

He first visited the orphanage where Mahesh had grown up. He met with the warden, the floor supervisors and the hygiene assistants. The warden shared that Mahesh sent a sizeable cheque every year and was an active participant in the activities held at the orphanage. The journalist also found out that Mahesh had a brother, Suresh, who now lived in the same shanty where the boys had grown up. Knowing that an interview with Suresh would create a powerful impact, he decided to make a meeting with Suresh his next stop.

The slum was now even larger and more notorious than what it had been 25 years back. There were open drains and floating filth, overflowing sewers and piles of dirt everywhere. The stench was overwhelming. The journalist waded his way through the dirt and the filth to Suresh's house. As he approached closer, he heard screams and ranting from within.

He peeped in and saw Suresh – uncouth, dirty, slobbering, cursing, abominably drunk – kicking his wife who was groaning on the floor of the dark, dinghy, unfurnished room. There were two children huddled in a corner with big dark sunken eyes, sobbing feebly. The journalist rushed forward to stop Suresh. "Stop it! Stop hitting your wife. Or else I will call the police". "Who the hell are you? This is my house, my wife and my life. Get out this instant", Suresh glared at the journalist as he drunkenly swayed on his feet. The journalist replied, "I am a journalist. And I came here to take your interview. You should be ashamed of yourself. What appalling circumstances you are in!! You are an animal. Why are you like this?"

Suresh glared at him, "I am like this because of my father. My father, a ruthless man, did not have anything but violence and hate in him. He was uneducated and never held a job in his entire life. He was a drunkard and used to hit my mother every day. I don't remember a single day when I wasn't thrashed by *him. I never received any love from him, so I don't even know what love is. I am like this because I wasn't exposed to or taught anything else. If my father hadn't been like that, I wouldn't be like this. Now get out before I throw you out of my house."*

The journalist left quietly, surreptitiously throwing a 500 rupee note to the wife on the floor, plagued by the hopeless, lifeless eyes of the woman on the floor and the children in the corner of the room, as he heard Suresh screaming, "I saw the money that he gave you, bitch. Give it to me right now."

Come Sunday, a very anxious journalist reached the house of Mahesh. It was a small bungalow in a good neighborhood. It was not extravagant, but it was neat and cozy. There was a small colorful garden outside the house. A young boy was teasing a small girl, presumably his sister, and the garden rang with the sounds of their squeals and laughter. A woman was standing at the window and she warned the boy, "Stop teasing your sister. Else I will tell your Papa." Though she was castigating her son, her voice was filled with pride and love because she knew that the most beautiful flowers in her garden were her children.

As the journalist reached the door, it swung open and he found himself staring at a well-dressed lady with bright eyes, shining hair rosy cheeks and a warm and open expression. She wasn't beautiful in the conventional sense, but her simplicity and her evident happiness more than made up for her plain features. There was a glow about her that even the most beautiful woman would have envied. "Come in. Come in. You must be the journalist who is here to write about my husband. Please have a seat while I arrange for tea and snacks. And you must have lunch with us," she smiled, as she ushered him into a neat and clean, well-lit room. As she hurried into the kitchen, the journalist came face to face with Mahesh.

Mahesh was not very tall, but could light up any room with his neatly combed hair, sparkling white clothes, welcoming smile and gentle eyes. The startled journalist, who was yet to recover from his meeting with Suresh the previous day, stuttered the first question that came to his mind. The same one that must have come to yours – "How come you have achieved so much in spite of your terribly humble beginnings?"

Mahesh smiled and pointed to a photo of a middle-aged man on the wall, which was decorated with a garland of fresh flowers and sweet smelling incense. "I am like this because of my Guru," he said. "Who is this Guru?" the journalist asked, staring at the photo, convinced that the man in the picture must be Mahesh's boss or maybe a Godfather or a Mentor, who had made him a icon.

"My Guru is my father," Mahesh said. And while the journalist stared in disbelief, Mahesh continued, "My father was a ruthless man, did not have anything but violence and hate in him. So, I have made a conscious effort never to hit and never to hate. He was uneducated and never held a job in his entire life. So, I have ensured that I never stop learning and have built my career with a single company. He was an alcoholic. I never drink because I have realized that drinking turns you into an animal. He used to hit my mother every day. I never lay a finger on my wife because I know that she is the only one who will stand by me through thick and thin. I don't remember a single day when I wasn't thrashed by my father. So, I never hit my children. I never received any love from him, so I know how a child yearns for his father's love. I spend a lot of time with my children assuring them of my love, and teaching them the most important lessons of life by being there for them. I am like this because of my father. If he hadn't been like that, I wouldn't be like this."

THE STORY OF TWO BROTHERS – DECODED

I am sure you are already realizing the truth. Or you wouldn't be looking as emotional as you are right now. Every time we tell this story in our training seminars or workshops, we see several people wiping their eyes. Isn't this the story, in slightly modified form, of every person who has a tough life?

I am like this because of my circumstances – if this were The Truth, how come we have so many people who have had phenomenal successes in spite of their extremely humble beginnings? Perhaps the answer lies in the fact that they have replaced the words 'because of' with 'in spite of'.

We come across thousands of people who have so much of talent, potential, intelligence and creativity – all wasted over a lifetime simply because they have been repeating this untruth.

The truth is – the only person stopping you is *you*. If you have truly made up your mind to be a success, there is honestly no one in the world who has the strength to stop you. But beware. The journey is not going to be easy. Your 'Yes' has to be stronger than the other person's 'No'.

Raqshit, Vijaya's son, recently lived this truth. He was studying at home for his examinations, when his friends called up and insisted that they 'group study'. He immediately packed his books and went to his friend's house to study with a few of his classmates. The result was that they were having too much fun to focus on the subject because of which he scored lower marks than expected. When his report card came, he had to confront the truth and this is what he said, "I made a mistake by opting for group study. I could have taken a stand and said that I prefer to study alone but I didn't. So, I am not going to blame my circumstances for getting lower scores. I take complete responsibility for this and I will get better scores next time."

That was a brave comment from a boy who is barely 13. We have always felt that children face up to 'The Truth' far more seamlessly than adults do.

It may takes months if not years for you to live the life that you want. And it will be a bloody fight for you, just as it was for Mahesh Sharma. But an easy fight never did make a legend, did it?

BREAK FREE TRUTH 1

I am like this because of ME.

BREAK FREE TRUTH 1 – IN A 'KICK ASS' FORMAT

This section is for the 'tough nuts' to crack – straight below the belt. This is for the ones who will read the story, shed a few tears and then go right back to saying, 'But my story is different. Mahesh Sharma was lucky.' Or some such crap.

In technical, psychological, behavioural language, these are called the ones with 'external locus of control, who exhibit repressed thoughts and submissive behaviour.' They are also called 'quitters', 'whiners', 'complainers', 'time-pass items' behind their back.

These are the people who really don't want advice or help. Whatever advice you give them, they have a reason why that can't be done. Let me give an example of a typical conversation with one of these 'I-am-like-this-because-of-others' people. Their sentences always start with a problem statement and – Surprise! – end with the same problem statement.

> *Here 'Q' stands for 'Quitter' not 'Questioner' and 'A' stands for 'Advisor' not 'Answerer'.*
>
> *Q – I want to lose weight, yaar. But I am unable to because my life is full of stress. You look so damn fit. Tell me how to become slimmer?*
>
> *A – You should go for walks in the morning. That's the best solution.*
>
> *Q – How to go for walks in the morning? There is absolutely no time. I have to cook, clean, pack lunch boxes, make breakfast, get the kids ready to go to school. Morning walks are impossible for me.*

A – *Then why don't you try to go for a walk after dinner?*

Q – *Arrey… no, yaar. I leave home early and come back really late. And I am dead tired at the end of the day. Walking in the night is out of question. And that's the only time I get to spend with the kids and my family. No. No, I am sure you can give me some other more effective solution. Please help me.*

A – *Looks like you have a very late dinner. Why don't you try having an early dinner?*

Q – *Early? And how do I manage that? I have to come early to eat early right? And my boss is a horror. He insists that I work late every day. It is impossible to leave on time. And the traffic. Don't ask! I reach back home an that's a miracle. So, early dinner is out of question.*

A – *Maybe you can start with something simple like having hot water with some lime juice first thing in the morning. It helps to cut fat, I believe.*

Q – *What? And not have tea? No, no. I simply can't function without my cuppa chai in the morning. Impossible.*

A – *Gym?*

Q – *Do you even know how much the gym costs? Too expensive. I had paid the monthly fees once last year. Went just twice. No time. What to do?*

A – *Salads?*

Q – *And who is going to make them for me? Husband wants this… son wants that. Daughter won't eat anything and mother-in-law has a special diet. I am sick of cooking. I can't cook one more variety every day. Impossible.*

A – *(now seriously confused and irritated) I don't know.*

> *Q - Ah! I told you. My life is full of stress. I want to lose weight, yaar. What to do? You look so damn fit. Tell me how to become slimmer?*

After reading this, you are either laughing or looking sheepish. The Qs don't want any advice. Told you. What they want is sympathy. Meaningless, mindless, supportive statements that help them feel connected to others like them. If the Advisor in the above case had been smart, the conversation would have been something like this –

Q - I want to lose weight, yaar. What to do? I am unable to because my life is full of stress. You look so damn fit. Tell me how to become slimmer?

A - You look fine. But you are right. Life is full of stress (with the appropriate tragic expression). How do you manage?

Q - What to do? Life is an endless journey of struggle. Children won't let me live in peace, husband won't let me die in peace. This is life. 'Zindagi ka safar... hai yeh kaisa safar... koi samjha nahi... koi jaana nahi'.

And if A sang it together with him/her, then even better.

If you really want to pass the time of the day, they are fantastic company. They can whine and complain endlessly. And their reply to your 'Hi! How's life?' will ensure that at least the next several hours is spent on how life *really* is. And if you are one of them, you will find a lot of solace. (After all who ever liked people who say 'Life is Awesome' anyway? Such types of people are anyway lying, right?)

So... Go on to the next page which has the Five Break Free Truths Tracker. Let your circumstances give you the leverage to become bigger, better, stronger, wealthier, more successful, more courageous and more fulfilled. All the best.

THE 5 BREAK FREE TRUTHS TRACKER - WEEK 1

Your Truth - I am like this because of my circumstances
The Truth - I am like this because of me

What I Believed – My Truth	*People around me are not supportive, so I am unable to achieve what I desire and what my potential is.*
What The Truth Is – My Realizations	*I have been saying this since the time I got married and have been lying to myself. The truth is I did not pursue my dreams with passion. If I had been persistent, I could have convinced everyone. My 'yes' was not stronger than their 'no'.*
My Next Step	*I am going to find a career counsellor for guidance on how to cover up for the lost years.* *I am going to apply for a job. Any job to start with.* *I am going to take this opportunity to become the best in what I do.*
My Truth Partner	*Prem Agarwal (Husband)*

THE 5 BREAK FREE TRUTHS TRACKER - WEEK 1

Your Truth - I am like this because of my circumstances
The Truth - I am like this because of me

What I Believed – My Truth	
What The Truth Is – My Realizations	

My Next Step	
My Truth Partner	

HOW OTHERS HAVE DISCOVERED THIS TRUTH

'My circumstances do not support me' ... that was the first reaction of Mr. Vaibhav Patel. He was responding to our question, 'What's stopping you, chief, from bringing your dreams into reality?'

Allow us to introduce Mr. Patel. He is the CMD of Kalpak Packaging Pvt. Ltd. (KPPL), a company that manufactures plastic packaging materials. With an annual sales turnover of about ₹20 crores and a steady list of clients, you would assume everything's just right for KPPL and Mr. Patel. But, that's not true. KPPL's annual turnover has been hovering around ₹20 crores for more than three years now. It appeared as if the organization had hit a block, like a steady moving ship that hits an iceberg and gets stuck, no movements ahead and no going back, just waiting for something to happen. To the goddamn iceberg! Mr. Patel's ship had hit an invisible iceberg, KPPL was neither growing nor losing out. It was just floating! That was when Mr. Patel became a part of our Executive Coaching Program for Business Owners and availed of our HRM Consultancy Services for KPPL.

When Mr. Patel got in touch with us through one of his friends who had successfully transformed his organization from a stuck boat to a sailing ship, he expected us to help him with the circumstances.

During our initial interactions with him, he shared his success story – his life was a rags-to-riches story. Most of his early life was shaped by decisions driven by poverty and basic needs for survival. He told us how he came from a small village in Kutchh (Gujarat) to join his uncle in Mumbai who was a hard-working plywood trader. He was then barely sixteen and had completed his tenth grade. It was here that he learnt his basics of entrepreneurship.

Vaibhav learnt the principles of hard work, honesty and commitment from his uncle. Through his dedication he earned his uncle's trust and that of other workers in his team. In just a few years, he was managing the entire operations for his uncle's business. He had become an expert in sales, customer service, despatches and cash flow management. His uncle too pampered him by entrusting him with newer and challenging tasks. While he completed his twelfth grade in Mumbai, he couldn't pursue his education further as the business took away most of his time and attention. He regretted the loss of this opportunity and until today feels he missed something important in his life.

It was during one of the visits to an exhibition organized by the All India Plastic Manufacturer's Association to which he had accompanied his uncle, that he was first exposed to the world of plastics. Taking up odd jobs in trading of plastic packaging materials, he learnt the nuances of manufacturing of plastic packaging materials. Having developed enough confidence and appropriate contacts in the industry, he ventured into manufacturing of plastic packaging with the blessings and financial backing of his uncle. This manufacturing unit was started in the backyard of his uncle's shop, a dingy

100 square feet room where only one small machine and two workers could work at a time. Thus, in just about ten years of his arrival in Mumbai – the City of Dreams, Vaibhav became an independent entrepreneur.

With his hard work and single-minded focus, the business took off in just a few years and soon had to be moved out to a bigger and better premise. Vaibhav chose an industrial area on the outskirts of Mumbai for setting up the larger unit. His new unit, named after his uncle Kalpakbhai Patel, had five machines and about twenty workers working in two shifts. Vaibhav himself would supervise the entire manufacturing process right from raw material inspection to processing and quality check of the finished goods. Since, he had hands-on expertise on every process and every machine, he was the single-point solution provider for his team. Between hectic production schedules, he would also make sales calls and meet up with all his clients personally and run back to the factory again to supervise the production. When he found himself short of managing the uncontrollable growth at KPPL, he requested his uncle to join him. Kalpakbhai was only too happy to accept. He had nearly lost interest in the plywood business after Vaibhav left to start on his own. The Chacha-Bhateeja (Uncle–Nephew) duo were a hit team. They understood each other well and led the team from the front. They complemented each other's strengths and also covered up well for each other's weaknesses.

KPPL bloomed under their leadership and became an established brand in the field of plastic packaging.

It was after twenty years of starting KPPL that we were sitting across Mr. Vaibhav Patel, now no more a lad of sixteen, but, a successful industrialist of about forty six years of age and thirty years of rich experience. While he shared his past,

Mr. Vaibhav Patel also shared his dreams for the future of KPPL. He shared that he wanted to see KPPL crossing a sales turnover of Rs. 100 crores annually, having factories and offices in various locations and amongst the leading brands in the plastics packaging industry. That's when we asked, 'What's stopping you from bringing your dreams into reality?' and his response was 'My circumstances do not support me.'

Mr. Patel had nearly two hundred employees now including workers and staff. But, he was completely tied up in operations. His hands-on experience and his ability to generate solutions which were his strengths in the early years of his business were acting as impediments for growth. He was generally the first to reach the office and mostly the last to leave. He was there in every department right where the action was.

During one of our initial diagnostic meetings, the purchase manager entered the room with a 'critical' problem. One of their main vendors was refusing to send the raw material and could he, "Vaibhavbhai, please speak to him because he would only send the material if you speak to him. Or else the production guys will be after my blood."

Mr. Patel, a man of action, and with the intention of proving to us, perhaps, about how it is impossible for him not to be involved, excused himself and then proceeded to make phone calls. He first called the vendor, then the accounts department as the supply was being held up because of delay in payment, then he called the vendor again, and convinced him that he would pay part of the sum owed by his company. He then called alternate vendors for a stop-gap arrangement, and then again the accounts department to coordinate the final terms.

I am sure you are curious about what the purchase manager was doing. We were too. To our amusement, the *purchase manager made himself comfortable in a chair. He took out his phone and started chatting on Whatsapp. (We could see this from where we were sitting). He then took a discreet selfie and uploaded it on his Facebook page. (He also showed us the photo for approval). He then spoke to his wife about the menu for dinner. And also called for a cup of tea for himself (Chhotu, ek cup kadak chai!) and for us (which we declined). Really! It was just too hilarious.*

After half an hour of frantic phone calls, the issue was finally sorted out. And the purchase manager left the room with a "You are awesome, Vaibhavbhai. If you hadn't been there this company would go to the dogs." A slightly smug Mr. Vaibhav Patel then said to us, "See I can't delegate to others. I don't have a powerful second line of leaders and whatever team I have is simply not competent enough. I have to get involved in the smallest of decisions. When you keep a control over things, they don't go haywire. I have learnt that from my uncle. People keep coming to me for approval on purchase decisions, production plans, despatch scheduling, transport decisions and even for matters like vacation and salary advances. Even if I delegate matters, things just come back to me and probably in a worse condition. So, it is better to take decisions at my level. I'm only a twelfth grader, so you see, recruiting highly qualified and professional staff is out of question. Besides, all clients want to interact with me directly. Unless I go personally and meet the decision makers, deals don't happen. I used to be so motivated many years ago. The circumstances have demotivated me completely. How and when do I think of the future of KPPL if I'm so engrossed in fire-fighting every day?"

Owing to these circumstances, Mr. Vaibhav Patel has never experienced a quality personal life. You can imagine the plight of this man when he asked 'Quality personal life, what's that?' With no holidays or break-away or rejuvenation time for himself, he simply does not have the bandwidth to think of creative ways to come out of this hole he has dug himself into. He is the same man who had defied his circumstances and shaped his career for thirty years! Being the intelligent reader that you are, we are sure you have already identified what ails Mr. Vaibhav Patel and KPPL.

You are right! It is not his circumstances that are stopping him from what he can become and to what heights he can take KPPL to! It is he, himself.

In the past three years that we have been working with Mr. Vaibhav Patel, our major energies were invested in making him realize that he was the biggest impediment to KPPL's growth. He felt that he was not delegating because his people were incompetent. But the truth was that his people were incompetent because he was not delegating work to them. He had never trained them personally to develop their competence, neither had he sent them for any training workshops. He felt that people were coming to him to get all the decisions approved by him because they didn't know how to take these decisions themselves.

But the truth was that people never learnt to take these decisions under him, because he never allowed them to. Unless people are empowered to take decisions, starting from the smaller ones to the bigger ones that impact larger scale operations and with reasonable freedom to make mistakes how are they going to learn the science of decision-making?

He believed that all decisions pertaining to employee affairs like leaves, salary advances, appraisals and promotions had to be taken by him because there was no standard policy document in the organization. The truth was that the standard policy document was never created because he was taking these decisions in any case.

He strongly believed that the customers disliked dealing with anyone else other than him. But the truth was he had not exposed his customers to newer and better faces other than him. He believed that he couldn't recruit highly qualified people because he himself was not very qualified. But the truth is, people don't follow your qualifications, they follow your values, your vision, your dreams and your ability to bring them to reality!

He believed that his circumstances had demotivated him. But, the truth was that he had allowed himself to be bogged down with his present challenges rather than get motivated with his future dreams. Thus, he had 'chosen' to be demotivated. He didn't go anymore to the office to fulfil his dreams or to become the person he was capable of becoming. Instead he was only going to the office to fight the day's challenge.

After initial resistance and denial (denial is the first response when people are shown the truth) that took a few months of counselling and coaching, Mr. Vaibhav Patel started seeing things from a different perspective. He started experimenting with delegation and empowerment as a tool for developing his people. He spent several hours with his key team members explaining how he took decisions and why he took them. When people came asking for decisions, he started counter-questioning them with the options they had thought of. This created a pressure on people to go to him with solutions and not just with problems.

At this juncture, he communicated to everyone that he would appreciate it if people came up with at least three different options to tackle any problem that they bring up to him. To ensure that he was taken seriously enough by his team-mates, he would send those coming up merely with problems back to their workplaces and ask them to come back only when they have thought of at least three solutions.

Although initially, there were several delays and a few errors arising out of this, a persistent mechanism of delegation-empowerment-feedback started paying off. Slowly yet surely, people started to take several decisions at their level. Although, Mr. Vaibhav Patel was still involved in bigger decisions, this in itself wasn't a small movement. To ensure that people had their eyes on the future while they took decisions in the present, he penned down the most important goals that he wanted KPPL to achieve. An organization-wide exercise was carried out to communicate these goals to each and everyone in the organization, in a language that they understood and in a manner in which they saw themselves playing some role in the achievement of those goals.

As the team went through several structured training workshops focused on developing their initiative and self-confidence, a culture of ownership was being born. The organization was slowly moving from being a 'one-man driven army' to a 'multiple-leader front'. A dedicated and customized 'Human Resources Management Policy' was designed for KPPL. It helped document all the decisions pertaining to vacation days, salaries, increments, promotions, organizational discipline, recruitments, employee career planning and employee resignations and many more. We didn't stop merely at creating the document, but also communicated the key points to the entire team through interactive training workshops. Feedback and comments were invited from the team and the team did come forward in sharing their thoughts. Some of these were actually incorporated in the policy document; some couldn't be as they were either impractical or potentially hazardous to the organization or the employees. The acceptance of this document by the entire team of two hundred people was a big relief to Mr. Vaibhav Patel as it meant freedom from the daily-decision making on matters pertaining to employee affairs.

The changes that have happened at KPPL are fantabulous. After three years, the organization posted a sales turnover of ₹38 crores and runs pretty much without Mr. Vaibhav Patel's direct involvement in most departments. Leaders seem to be shaping up in various departments as one gets to hear stories of various 'innovators' in the team. But the most inspiring change that's happened is in the outlook of Mr. Vaibhav Patel.

In a recent Annual Strategy Meeting where his entire team was giving presentations on the plans for the coming year, a Sales Manager commented that "Circumstances in my area are not conducive to our business. The market is too tough and the competition is killing. My team is pretty demotivated. We'll have to wait for the circumstances to improve. So, this year we would either maintain our last year's performance or go for a 20% lower target than the last year."

Mr. Vaibhav Patel smiled at the Sales Manager and said, "Instead of waiting for the circumstances to improve, maybe you should focus on improving your approach. If your team is demotivated, it is not because of the challenging circumstances. Rather, you made your circumstances challenging by being demotivated. You are de-motivated because you have chosen to be demotivated!"

Wow! One life touched, one life transformed! Every time that happens, both of us give each other a 'taali' (the 'high-five' as they call it). There are more than 6 billion people on this planet. Every 'taali' means, one down with a lie... only 5,99,99,99,999 people more to go! Yay!

FACING THIS TRUTH RIGHT NOW

John Maxwell in his book *21 Irrefutable Laws of Leadership* says the following about "The Law of Respect":

> *People don't follow others by accident. They follow individuals whose leadership they respect. Someone who is an 8 in leadership (on a scale from 1 to 10, with 10 being the strongest) doesn't go out and look for a 6 to follow – he naturally follows a 9 or 10. The less skilled follow the more highly skilled and gifted. Occasionally, a strong leader may choose to follow someone weaker than himself. But when that happens, it's for a reason. For example, the stronger leader may do it out of respect for a person's office or past accomplishments. Or he may be following the chain of command. In general though, followers are attracted to people who are better leaders than themselves. That is the Law of Respect.*

The question to ask ourselves is then, 'How do I gain respect? By allowing my circumstances to control me or by taking control of them?' Respect is earned when we take control of our circumstances. We haven't heard of successful men whose circumstances were easy. In fact, each success story is filled with pages and pages of descriptions of tough circumstances, of the struggle to come to terms with those circumstances, of the identification of opportunity in those circumstances and of the victory over those circumstances.

> *Interestingly, John Maxwell's book was gifted to Vijaya by our ex-boss and one of our Gurus Mr. Santosh Nair. He was a strong leader and had earned our following through respect. We saw our 'Mahesh Sharma' in him – the ability to identify opportunity in tough circumstances and gaining victory*

over those circumstances. A few months ago, when Vijaya was selected by Loksatta (a leading Marathi daily by the Indian Express Group) *for the Navadurga Award, they ran a half-page cover-story on her. Most of the story covered her difficult childhood, her struggle against poverty while gaining academic excellence, her topping university while managing a kid and home, her journey as a first-generation entrepreneur, her struggle to establish herself as an HR Consultant of repute in an extremely male-dominated world and her struggle to create a sustainable organization. While this took away 95 percent of the article space, her success was summed up in one single paragraph. As the cover story got printed, she received thousands of phone calls, SMSs, emails from all across the state of Maharashtra, literally thousands. People called up from metro cities and from the remotest of villages, the old ones called, the young ones too, teachers called, doctors called, business owners called, government employees called, students called and homemakers called. It was like a tsunami of phone calls that just wouldn't stop. She still receives stray calls from people who have read that article. What did all these people call her for? Was it to feel sorry that she had a tough childhood or that she didn't have the 'right circumstances'? No... absolutely not!*

All those people called to congratulate her because she identified opportunity in her tough circumstances and emerged victorious. They called because they saw a ray of hope for themselves; because they felt inspired. They saw their 'Mahesh Sharma' in her. A teacher from a remote village in Latur called to tell her that she had just read out her article to her class of sixth graders and several students said that they too will fight their circumstances and succeed one day. A homemaker from Nagpur who had given up on life called to tell her that after reading the article, she has decided to take up a job and become financially independent. An uneducated sweeper from a Medical Hospital in Pune called to say, "I will now work very hard, study very hard and one day I will become the Administrative In-charge of our Hospital".

Vijaya says, "The irony of the world is that it is full of heroes. And yet, it needs more!" Yes, the world needs more heroes. It always did.

How does one become a hero? Want to know? Read on!

The Birth of the Hero in You

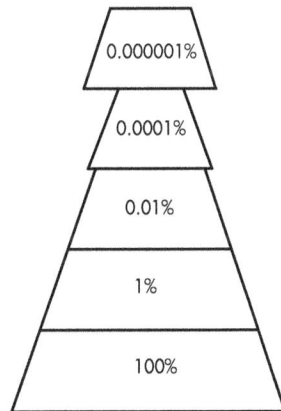

A hero is someone who inspires others to live a life of freedom, prosperity, personal values and a life of contribution. Every society needs heroes – they are the ones who inspire others to a better life, a life worthy of being lived and emulated. A society without heroes is like a body without a soul. These are the people who understand the 'Process of Celestial Selection'. Atheists… hold it! Don't turn the page please. By *Celestial* we don't mean *Godly*, we mean a sum

Narrate Your Success Story To The World

↑

Script Your Success Story

↑

Identify Opportunities

↑

Thank The Selector

↑

Identify Your Tough Circumstances

| 0.000001% |
| 0.0001% |
| 0.01% |
| 1% |
| 100% |

Birth of a Hero   No. of People at Various Stages

total of all those incidents and events that chose you to face the tough circumstances. Yes, we believe the ones who face adversity are the "truly chosen" ones, just that the heroes realise it and the non-heroes don't!

1. Identify Your Tough Circumstances – 100 percent of people know how to do this. Most of us have faced tough circumstances – either we didn't receive the right parenting, the right schooling, the right physique, the right environment, the right job, the right boss, the right customers…the list is endless! The successful and the not-so-successful people have faced tough circumstances alike. Then, what's the difference between the two?

2. Thank The Selector – The difference between the super-successful and the not-so-successful is that the latter look at the challenging circumstances and yell out aloud at people around 'But, why me?' Whereas the former i.e. the super-successful look at the challenging circumstances, take a deep breath, look at the sky and scream at the top of their voice, "Thank you! Thank you for choosing me!" Our experience of working with people has taught us that hardly one percent of people graciously accept the challenges thrown at them.

3. Identify Opportunities – There are still lesser number of people who, having accepted the challenging circumstances, are able to identify opportunities hidden beneath the challenges. This is typically that area of work in which you are good at.

We founded Liberation Coaches in 2006 and things went pretty well for the first two years of our operations (notwithstanding the fact that we started in Amol's rented apartment, sitting on the floor, where 9 other inmates already lived and we had no laptop or computers to work on, the first laptop was bought only after our first client paid us in advance for HRM Consulting Services!). From a friends-only team of three people in 2006, we became a fifteen-member professional team in 2008. In 2007, we bought a second-hand car and in 2008, our first office. This was about the time we were managing nearly eighteen mid-sized organizations as clients in training and consultancy services and two large multinationals in training services. That included Mahindra & Mahindra, a client we are hugely indebted to.

And then, the recession hit the market. We didn't think it would affect us, after all we were the good guys! But, as clients started defaulting on payments and cancelling training workshops, we pretty soon realized what we were up to! In a span of three months, sixteen mid-sized companies 'took a break' from the consultancy services and two multinationals wrote to us communicating 'training budgets frozen'. Mahindra & Mahindra continued with its annual training schedule.

We had fifteen mouths to feed, office EMIs to pay and other overheads to take care of. We had no savings – whatever savings we had made in the last two years were invested in the purchase of the new office. We had been teaching others to fight, so we were not going down without a good fight! Months went by without any income and as funds from family and friends went dry, things started looking bleak.

That's when the NMIMS University offered a teaching assignment to Vijaya, who had completed her MBA from there. She was to conduct a course of ten lectures on Organizational Behaviour for two batches of their students who were doing their MBA – Family Managed Business Program. When they needed a faculty for teaching a course on Sundays to the students of the Distance Learning Program, Vijaya recommended me (Amol). Suddenly, a whole new market of opportunities opened up, which we grabbed with both hands.

We sent our bio-data to several institutes and many of them wrote back, thus opening the doors to us teaching as visiting faculty in several leading management institutes! The remuneration was paltry compared to what we charged as trainers and consultants to the corporate world. We couldn't generate our salaries. But it helped us survive and pay the salaries of our people on time. Needless to say, it was an enriching experience for both – us and the students. The students enjoyed our lectures because we brought 'real-life' examples to the classroom having worked closely with the corporate sector and dozens of family businesses. For us, this was definitely an opportunity in disguise as we were forced to read and refresh several management concepts again. And the added bonus of interacting with young and bright minds! We delivered lectures seven days a week, including Sundays; at times these lectures stretched non-stop from 6.30 am to 10.00 pm.

4. Script Your Success Story – Once you have identified the opportunity, you just have to get going. The secret lies in doing more of what you are good at. For us, it was teaching. What's it going to be for you?

A fantastic human being we know of is Dr. Ashok Khanvte; a Mumbai-based preventive health-care specialist, a motivational speaker par excellence, an adventure enthusiast, a marathon runner, an avid mountaineer and one of our Gurus. Dr. Khanvte is a surgeon by qualification and had a roaring practice in the heart of the city. When everything seemed to be going well, he suffered a paralytic stroke at forty-seven. He survived the stroke, but with a severe side-affect—the surgeon's hands couldn't stay steady! Years of medical practice and a devoted set of clientele... all but worthless in one night!

Most of us would have said 'Why me?' But, not this doctor. He focused all his energies on preventive healthcare and giving 'Health-Talks' to various organizations. Impressed by his 'Health-Talks', several leading banks and multinationals invited him as their Medical Consultant. Today he is an extremely busy doctor and at 67 runs four marathons a year. He has scripted his success story!

Scripting your success story simply means identifying what you're good at and using it as an opportunity to overcome your challenging circumstances. It is doing what is right, whether the circumstances are right or not. Or rather we should say, it is doing what is right especially when the circumstances are not right! And doing it every day, without fail, till the time the 'tough circumstances' seem 'pretty easy to handle!'

When a salesman goes into the field every day (in spite of) knowing that the market is tough, he is scripting his success story. When a production manager continues to produce (in spite of) knowing that he doesn't have the best machines or the best workforce, he is scripting his success story. When a housewife keeps applying to various organizations (in spite of) knowing that her chances of selection are weak, she is scripting her success story. When a student keeps walking to a school which is a long way from his home every day (in spite of) knowing that his father may not be able afford higher education tomorrow, he is scripting his success story. When a teacher continues teaching at her best every day (in spite of) knowing that several students may not like studying at all, she is scripting her success story. When a business owner follows the principles of honest business and non-acceptance of cash every day (in spite of) knowing that others don't care, he is scripting his success story. When a committed police officer investigates every case upholding the spirit of law (in spite of) knowing that superiors may not care, he is scripting his success story. So... what's your story?

5. Narrate Your Success Story – It is not merely enough to script a success story, not enough to live like a hero. It is equally essential to narrate the story to others – to inspire others, to show them the light, to give them a ray of hope. Remember, Prince Siddhartha came back after he became the 'Buddha'. He shared. Mahatma Gandhi shared, Swami Vivekananda shared, Jawaharlal Nehru shared, Amitabh Bachchan shared, Sachin Tendulkar shared, Dr. APJ Abdul Kalam shared and hundreds of other kind men and women shared their stories of struggle with and triumph over circumstances. Some heroes have narrated their stories through their writings, some through interviews given to various people, some through their seminars and talks the medium doesn't matter. But, if you have lived the life of a hero, it's your duty to share it with others!

But beware, not just you, others must feel you've lived the life of a hero. That means you must have gone through stages one to four first before you attempt to 'narrate your story'. Otherwise, yeah, yeah, you know what will happen!

- Would you like to have a life of achievement like Mahesh Sharma?
- Would you like to see your challenges getting converted into your opportunities?
- Would you like to transform yourselves from a hapless 'victim of circumstances' to 'creator of your destiny'?
- Would you like to see growth and success like Mr. Vaibhav Patel?
- Would you like to feel in control of your destiny RIGHT NOW?

LIVING THE TRUTH RIGHT NOW

On the next page, write at least five tough/challenging circumstances that you are going through or have gone through.

The circumstances you have faced may be personal like 'I had a tough childhood' or 'I went to a vernacular medium school and feel unsure in front of the city-bred boys' or 'I come from a middle class background, hence find it difficult to interact with high-ranking officials.' The circumstances you have faced might also be related to the outside world like, 'the market is very tough', or 'my competition is killing me' or 'politics is rampant in my organization'. Write in your own words, in a language that you prefer. The next column is where you 'Thank the Selector'. Doesn't matter who the selector was, or what you call him / her. This is the step where you 'accept the circumstances wholeheartedly' as if they were especially custom-made for you, as if you placed an order and someone tailored these challenges for you, as if you had been waiting for a challenge as worthy as the one you are facing right now! So say, 'thank you, thank you for choosing me!' Say it with all your heart. Write it with all the conviction you got. You, and only you on this entire planet were selected to be worthy of this challenge!

Now identify the opportunities you have. Remember there's always an opportunity lying beneath the big scary challenge! Find it, search for it. Keep searching for it till you are convinced that this opportunity will help you overcome the challenging circumstance you are faced with. For the student who's walking to school every day, the opportunity might be 'an extremely hard to earn a scholarship for higher studies'. For the salesman who's facing a tough market, the opportunity might be 'start my day early, meet more people, learn to handle objections professionally and increase sales figures'. For the homemaker faced with the daunting task of applying for and facing interviews, the opportunity might be 'start tuition classes at home to regain my confidence and develop my communication skills'.

The fourth column 'Scripting My Success Story' is where you write your action plan on how exactly you are going to use the opportunity just identified. So, what are you waiting for! There's no going to the next section unless your *Personal Guide to Heroism* is complete! Go on… get going!

Best of luck!

MY PERSONAL GUIDE TO HEROISM

My Tough Circumstances	Let Me Thank The Selector	Opportunities I Have	Scripting My Success Story

2

Your Truth

2

I would rather stay the way I AM!

Why are people so stubborn?
I have such fantastic ideas, my boss refuses to adopt them..
You don't get committed employees nowadays.
My father is hopeless. The world has changed, but he refuses to.
My co-Director is such an adamant fellow, he just won't take any
*   feedback from me.*
Clients don't pay on time nowadays, they just don't honour our
*   credit policy.*
My wife is still the same, she hasn't learned anything since we married.
I am so hard working but I have such lazy subordinates…
Why won't people accept me the way I am? I know better than so
*   many members of my team. Yet they won't follow me.*
My brother-in-law has no idea how to run his business. He should
*   take some lessons from me.*
I am such a good leader, if only my people could see it.
I am such a good husband, my wife doesn't know how lucky she is.
Training workshops? For me? Ha, ha… good joke! Send the trainer
*   to me… I'll teach him a thing or two!*
What are consultants going to tell me about my business that I
*   already don't know?*
I would rather not change anything about myself.
I am who I am. Why should I be any different?
People who change are not to be trusted.

If the above is you, welcome to the 'I-would-rather-be-the-way-
I-am' club!' There are millions of members in this club. They are

easily recognizable. They are in love with themselves and love every opportunity to give *gyaan* to others. Most members of this club are pretty self-satisfied as they truly believe that they know quite a lot about the world and its affairs and that everyone else needs education.

These are people who find faults in the market (customers are too demanding, they don't pay in time, they only want to pay in cash, they're unrealistic etc.), in their team (if only I could get a more competent team, there's no commitment in my people, you don't get hardworking people nowadays etc.), in their family (my wife is so stubborn, I didn't get the right support from my father, I am so much better than my brother but he doesn't understand it etc.) and everything else that is outside of them (taxes are so damn high, the infrastructure in our state is so poor, our vendors are so unprofessional, my company policy is biased etc.).

Are you an active member of this club? Perhaps, you became a member when you started achieving. For many of us, the feeling grew as we realized that we have achieved more than many of our counterparts or classmates or relatives. It is therefore that they believe that they must share their 'rich advice' with people. Many a times, members of this club are 'gifted' with sycophants around them who contribute to the inflation of their egos! So while these people are capable of achieving far more and scaling great heights of success, they become complacent with their miniscule achievements.

What's Your Story?
Below this paragraph, you will find a table that is designed to enable you to face Your Truth.

Step 1
The Belief – Pick out one or similar sentences from the previous page that you have been uttering or thinking regularly.

Step 2
The Evidence – Write down at least one evidence of why those sentences have been repeated by you so often.

Step 3
The Outcome – Write your feelings when you have 'proved' that the sentences are your life's Truth.

The Belief ...	The Evidence ...

The Outcome ...

Step 4
Read on...

THE STORY OF NARCISSUS – FROM GREEK MYTHOLOGY

We love mythological tales. Tales of Demons and Angels, of Gods and Goddesses, of Vampires and Ghosts. Mythology has always reminded us of our childhood when we would huddle up in cold winters under a single blanket, and listen wide-eyed as our mothers and grandmothers wove colourful stories of the impossible. This story is about a Greek God – Narcissus.

Narcissus was the son of Cephissus, the River God and the most beautiful sylph (fairy), Liriope. Before Narcissus was born, Liriope was visited by an astrologer, who predicted that Narcissus would enjoy a long life if he did not discover himself. Perhaps that is why Liriope ensured that there was not a single mirror or surface that could reflect the image of her unborn son even before the day he was born.

Finally Narcissus was born. And he was incredibly beautiful. He had big, expressive, deep-set hazel eyes speckled with the green of the forest and the blue of the ocean. He had a long straight nose and luscious red lips, within which white even teeth shone every time he smiled. He had curly, shiny, auburn hair that surrounded his head like an Angel's halo and his skin was like cream with the palest shade of rose.

He grew into a tall, robust youth. His body was well-built with wide shoulders and chest, strong arms, a narrow waist, long, muscular legs and a deep resonant voice. He was the epitome of all men and there was seldom a person, man or woman, who did not fall in love with him on sight, as he freely roamed the forests and the mountains, growing more handsome every day.

Echo, the daughter of Hermes, was one such maiden who was madly in love with Narcissus. Echo was beautiful. She had dark, expressive, doe-like eyes framed with thick lashes, rose bud lips, long black hair that flew like the wind and skin the colour of honey. She had been playing in the mountains with her friends once, when Narcissus happened to pass that way, looking for wild flowers and fruits. It was love at first sight for her, like it was for many others in the land.

Echo was also the companion of Hera, Lord Zeus's wife. Echo had the gift of the gab and entertained Hera throughout the day with amusing stories and anecdotes. One day, Hera discovered that Zeus had commanded Echo to keep Hera busy so that he could spend his time romantically wooing other celestial maidens. Hera was furious at Echo for misleading her and hiding the truth behind what she believed were flattery and lies. She cursed Echo by taking away her voice. "You love talking, don't you?" she hissed angrily, "Then that's what I will take away from you. Henceforth, you will only be able to utter a single word at a time. And because you are too glib with words, you will never be able to weave sentences again and misguide someone else. The only word you will be able to speak is the last word of what someone has spoken to you. No go away. And enjoy your silence while I face mine." And Hera turned her back and stalked away, leaving a teary and terrified Echo behind.

A dispirited Echo was wandering in the forest, when she saw Narcissus in the distance. But she couldn't utter a word because of Hera's curse! And she was ashamed of the fact that she couldn't speak to him. So, she followed Narcissus from a distance waiting for an opportunity to open her heart to him. After some time Narcissus stopped by a river to drink water. That was the first time Narcissus saw his own reflection. And he fell in love... with himself.

"Hello!'" said Narcissus to his own reflection.

"Hello... Hello... Hello..." Echo, who had been hiding behind a tree, repeated.

Narcissus smiled at his reflection, which smiled at him right back.

"I want to meet you." said Narcissus to the image.

"Meet you, meet you, meet you.' repeated Echo.

'Can you come here?' Narcissus asked.

'You come here. You come here. You come here,' Echo said in her sweet melodious voice.

An eager Narcissus jumped into the river to meet his love… his own reflection! Finding nothing in the water, he climbed out. He looked again into the river and saw himself in it.

"Are you playing with me?" he asked his reflection.

"Playing. Playing. Playing," Echo replied back.

He kept talking to his reflection. Echo kept repeating his words thereby adding to his confusion and despair. He would jump into the water thereby breaking his own image into a million scattered stars. He would then climb back to the bank and there his reflection was in the water, looking beautiful, inviting and eager.

The more he saw himself, the more Narcissus fell madly in love. He lost all sense of reality. For the entire day he sat gazing at and calling out to his reflection till the sun set in the sky and the reflection was no longer visible. Thinking that his love had gone home, he wandered throughout the night looking for him in the villages around the forest. "Have you seen the love of my life?" he asked the villagers with tears in his eyes, 'the one with the big eyes, the long hair, the beautiful smile?' "Who are you looking for? Do you have a name?" the kind-hearted villagers asked Narcissus who was looking even more beautiful in his despair. "No," the confused Narcissus whispered, "But my love is difficult to miss."

The villagers pointed out many beauties to him, but he just shook his head, tears spilling out of his eyes as he walked towards the next village where the process of looking for his love started again. And then the next and the next till it was dawn, his hope turning to anxiety and then to abject misery. "Maybe you will find your love in the same place again tomorrow morning, son," suggested an old villager.

Narcissus rushed back to the river as it was breaking dawn and there his love was, exactly where he had left him. He smiled happily and his image smiled back at him. He never saw Echo who had been following him with a heart filled with love and a tongue that refused to help her express it. And then the cycle started all over again. Narcissus talking to himself, Echo repeating his words, him jumping into the water, his reflection exploding into a million fragments, him climbing back to the bank, looking at himself, falling in love all over again, Narcissus talking to himself, Echo repeating his words... you get the picture. This continued until night, when the reflection would disappear in the darkness. Narcissus, again wandered to the villages and with growing despondency begged the villagers to help him find his love. In the morning he was back at the river waiting for his love to show up. Echo, saw his futile attempts and walked up to him to help him, but she had no words and Narcissus had no patience. He saw her as an interruption and shooed her away as he went back to gazing at himself.

Days, weeks and then months passed by. Narcissus was so obsessed in his love that he forgot to eat, sleep, drink and soon grew weak. He lost the glow from his cheeks and the sheen from his hair. His body became thin and riddled with illness. But he never saw it. He was blinded by his love for himself and it led him to his deathbed.

Echo sat close to him, helplessly watching the love of her life wither away. And one day, Narcissus was dead. His once beautiful body was reduced to soil. From this soil by the river bank rose a beautiful flower. Echo died unable to bear the loss

> *of her love and what remained of her was only her yearning spirit, wandering the mountains, looking for a way to express her unfulfilled love. Even today, when we shout into the mountains, you will hear Echo speaking back to you.*
>
> *This flower that grows by the side of the river, is now termed "Narcissus", because it looks as though it is gazing at itself. Perhaps you know it by its more common name "Nargis".*

"Narcissism" is also a term used in psychology to denote a personality disorder that stems from obsessive love for oneself.

And people who are excessively in love with themselves and their own ideas are termed as "narcissists"!

THE STORY OF NARCISSUS – DECODED

All normal human beings have an 'ego' or 'sense of self'. It is what makes them learn and progress and achieve. It is what gives them an identity and makes them unique amongst the millions of others on this planet. The very fact that no two human beings are the same is nature's way of supporting that 'ego' and 'sense of self'.

But the problem arises when our 'ego' becomes bigger than our 'self' – like Narcissus. He fell so much in love with himself without even realizing it, that he lost his grip on reality and eventually his life. And like Narcissus, many of us are so much in love with ourselves that we lead ourselves to our own destruction. We come across these kinds every day in our training programs and seminars. They come there with deep scepticism and suspicion of anyone or anything that is not in sync with what they believe in. And that is their approach to life too. They refuse to face reality and also the reality about themselves. Even the fact that they have failed in their career and relationships does not make them pause and reconsider. They live their past glory over and over again, falling more in love with who they could be and were, rather than who they are. And just like Narcissus, they become weaker and more insignificant by the day simply because they did not pause to align themselves with the present truth about themselves.

If Narcissus had seen himself, unblended by his obsessive love, he would have identified the first warning signs of deterioration. He would have tried to understand what Echo was trying to tell him instead of shooing her away. He would have taken proactive steps to rebuild his strength, his body, his beauty. But he was too much in love to 'see'.

When you meet people who have achieved super success, you will always find them very grounded and humble. They are willing to learn. They are willing to change. They are open to newer ideas. They are more alert to the environment. They have a dispassionate view of themselves. And that helps them to sense the need for change even before it actually occurs. Or maybe it is the other way around – they are all this and that is why they have achieved super success.

BREAK FREE TRUTH 2

*If I Stay the Way I am
I will Stay Where I am*

BREAK FREE TRUTH 2 – IN A 'KICK-ASS' FORMAT

Warning! Not for the faint-hearted. And NO. Don't blame us if you burst a blood vessel while reading this. This one is going to be really painful.

You were reading this book so that you could give this *gyaan* to someone, right? As you were reading about Narcissus, you laughed at how apt a description it was about that idiot of a boss/subordinate/client/customer/uncle, right? Because this story was especially for 'the other idiots' around you, but not for you, right? Wrong. This truth was especially customized for you.

So, you think you are perfect. Then how come you are not the Managing Director of an MNC? Or the owner of a 10000 crore company? Or the President of the country? If you are saying 'it is because of others', then go back to Story 1. You have learnt nothing there.

Here is a dialogue reproduced verbatim for you between two people who are talking about a member of the 'I-would-rather-be-the-way-I-am' club. You are going to love it. –

R – Hiya! Why you looking so depressed?

M – I am supposed to meet my boss today for a meeting.

R – And that is bad?

M – I get depressed at the thought of meeting him. I think he is a pain in the ass. I don't like his know-it-all-attitude. I am sick of his gyaan.

R - It can't be that bad.

M - It is worse. He makes my life miserable. I swear that if I could be forgiven one murder, then I won't take a moment to send him, snivelling, (Snivelling here would mean - making one cry so much that gloop is leaking from one's nose - the greenish yellow sticky kind) to hell. I simply am waiting for a transfer to another planet, city, organization or at least department, so I don't have to be around him.

We guess, you kind of got the gist of what we are saying. Or rather what others are thinking.

So you want to know how to get out of this? The top five things you can do today.

1. **LISTEN.** Not just hear. Listen. Both to what people are saying and also to what people are NOT saying.
2. **STOP TALKING.** Stuff your mouth with paper. Do *anything* to make sure that your contribution to conversations is never more than 30 percent.
3. **PROBE.** Ask questions. Not the ones that would corner the other guy. But those that will inspire him / her to think and share and innovate and participate.
4. **LEARN.** About people. The truly great ones. The role models that are generally accepted as such by people. And copy their behaviour - their humility, passion, their ability to inspire others and their leadership qualities.
5. **WRITE A BOOK.** *Like us, about all the gyaan you have.* Or blogs and articles about your experiences and what you have learned from them. That way, you will be sharing your thoughts, but the choice of subscribing to those thoughts will rest with others.

Done? So, go on. Fill in the Tracker. And make sure you have an open mind. Because one doesn't want to destroy oneself by refusing to change like Narcissus, right? Especially when you have the potential to become even more dynamic, competent, confident and successful than you are now. All the best.

THE 5 BREAK FREE TRUTHS TRACKER – WEEK 2

Your Truth – I would rather stay the way I am

The Truth – If I stay the way I am, I will stay where I am

What I Believed – My Truth	I have always blamed others for not changing. I thought I was perfect. And used to get really angry at people for not agreeing with whatever I said. I thought they were stubborn.
What The Truth Is – My Realizations	A painful truth for me is that people are only as stubborn as I am. Why should someone agree with what I say, when I don't agree with what they say? I am not perfect. It is foolish of me to think that I don't need to change at all.
My Next Step	Every time I disagree with someone, I am going to pause. I am going to sincerely try to see it from their point of view. If I don't agree to their thought, I am going to respectfully agree to disagree. I will get a personal coach to help me work on my areas of change.
My Truth Partner	Abhijeet Mane (My best friend)

THE 5 BREAK FREE TRUTHS TRACKER – WEEK 2

Your Truth – I would rather stay the way I am

The Truth – If I stay the way I am, I will stay where I am

What I Believed – My Truth	
What The Truth Is – My Realizations	
My Next Step	
My Truth Partner	

HOW OTHERS AROUND YOU HAVE DISCOVERED THIS TRUTH

This is the case of Mr. Shyam Agarwal (name changed), a cloth merchant. He is a distributor with AVN Textiles Limited, a Mumbai-based firm that manufactures men's suiting and shirting. He has spent twenty years in this business and manages the entire Delhi and NCR (National Capital Region) for AVN Textiles. He is quite a well-known personality in his market and owing to his affable manner, quite liked too.

Mr. Agarwal is a successful man you see, he does a sales turnover of around ₹10-12 crores every year. He has four people on his staff (two accountants, an office attendant and a driver), owns a big 3-bedroom apartment in the heart of Delhi, drives a Honda City and spends a lot of quality time with his family. In a training workshop we conducted about a year ago for all the Distributors of AVN Textiles on how to multiply their sales figures; this is how a conversation with him unfolded–

Shyam Agarwal – Okay all that is fine…we'll go and multiply the sale! That's not a problem… in fact it is the easiest part! Go into the market and dump more on your retailers… I have already done all that…

Amol Muley (interrupting) – Hold it sir… we never said anything about 'dumping'… we used the term 'selling'.

Shyam Agarwal – Yeah, okay, one and the same thing!

Amol Muley – No sir… definitely not! There is way too much difference between the two terms… the attitude, the meaning; the philosophies behind the two terms are vastly different. Dumping is done to fulfil one's target without consideration for the other party. Whereas selling is a process of identifying people's needs and providing solutions accordingly. Dumping creates strain in relationships whereas selling enhances results and relationships both. People indulge in dumping only because they haven't learned the science of sales.

Shyam Agarwal – Yeah ok, whatever the word for it is, that's not the issue. The issue is something else.

Vijaya Suvarna – What is the issue then?

Shyam Agarwal – See, our retailers and wholesalers don't pay on time. What's the point of multiplying our business if we are not going to get our money on time?

Vijaya Suvarna – Would you please elaborate?

Shyam Agarwal – I mean, they don't pay within the credit period. We are already cash-strapped. Increasing the business further will only drive us to the corner.

Amol Muley – What is the credit period you offer?

Shyam Agarwal – 60 days.

Amol Muley – And when do your retailers pay you Mr. Agarwal?

Shyam Agarwal – Most of them are pay after six months. Only a few pay between three to four months. Not even one retailer pays within 60 days.

Vijaya Suvarna – So what do you do when they don't pay you within 60 days?

Shyam Agarwal – What can I do? There are too many suppliers and too many textile mills now. The retailers are not dependent on me, I am dependent on them. If I pressurize them to pay within 60 days or take any penal action like charging interest on the outstanding amount, they simply ask me to take back the stock and threaten never to buy again from me.

Amol Muley – Hmm. Is it the first time they have done this to you?

Shyam Agarwal – No, that's what they have been doing for nearly ten years now! They know my weak spots pretty well.

Vijaya Suvarna – Oh great! That's good news!

Shyam Agarwal – Good news? How come?

Vijaya Suvarna – Well, you see they have been delaying payments for a decade now. So their behaviour doesn't come as a shock to you. Right? Now that's the good news! So, after a decade of experience one is expected to be prepared with a strategy to combat a recurring situation. Since in this case the retailers are delaying payments every time, that's your recurring situation. And you got a decade-long experience of facing it. So, what's your strategy to overcome the situation?

Shyam Agarwal – Strategy?! Why should I have a strategy? See my problem is that retailers do not pay on time.

Amol Muley – And how long have you known it?

Shyam Agarwal – 10 years…

Amol Muley – Exactly our point! So what have you done in these 10 years to overcome the situation?

Shyam Agarwal – ………………..

Vijaya Suvarna – Have you read any book on negotiations? Or on the art of collecting money on time?

Shyam Agarwal – No….

Amol Muley – Have you attended any training workshop on Credit Collections or Collections Management?

Shyam Agarwal – Er… no, you see, theory doesn't help… I'm talking of practical challenges here.

Amol Muley – Theories are not made up in the stars, sir. They are derived on the basis of most successful approaches followed by the most successful people. Which theories on sales and collections have you read to find them impractical?

Shyam Agarwal – Well, I don't need to read anything. I know everything about my business.

Vijaya Suvarna – Everything? Are you sure, Sir? Then how come you have outstandings beyond six months?

Shyam Agarwal – But that's because the retailers do not change their ways. They act very pricey nowadays.

Vijaya Suvarna – So all the retailers are at fault. There is nothing wrong with our approach? Nothing that can be improved?

Shyam Agarwal – ....

Amol Muley – How many retailers do we have in the Delhi and NCR sir?

Shyam Agarwal Considering all of them together, the small, large and the larger chains... say about two thousand five hundred to three thousand retail stores is what we have. However, our active buyers are about two hundred to two-hundred and fifty retailers. And I don't intend to recruit more retailers.... who knows they might be worse!

Amol Muley – Hmm. So, is it intelligent to change the attitude of three thousand retailers or is it more fruitful to change our approach of collecting money?

Shyam Agarwal – (after a long pause) Hmm! You have a point there! I get it. But, what do I change? What do you suggest?

Vijaya Suvarna – We suggest a one-to-one meeting with your Business Coach to discuss various aspects of your challenge and the possible solutions.

Shyam Agarwal – But, I don't have a Coach.

Vijaya Suvarna – Okay. Meet us after the training session is over. Let's chat.

~

In a conversation that lasted less than ten minutes, Mr. Agarwal moved from the closed-door attitude of 'I-know-everything' to the open-minded attitude of 'may-be-there's-something-more'. In his belief that he knew everything, he was expecting the world around him to change, while he stayed the way he was. He expected his retailers to start paying in time, while he and his team did nothing to make them pay on time. Owing to this, the delays in the outstanding amount became a regular affair and the outstanding amount kept piling up. Nothing moved in this aspect, like our truth says, 'If you stay the way you are, you will stay where you are!'

This conversation created an openness to change in the mind of Mr. Agarwal and the desire to look at things differently. But mind you, it has only created the openness to change, the real change hasn't happened yet! Want to know what happened next? Read on!

We believe that those who have the capability to identify problems also have the capability of identifying the solutions. Our coach (well... you see, we too have a Business Coach. And his name is Mr. Pramod Gothi, the founder of North Star Advisors and Business Coach to India's leading Business Houses), has always maintained that 'Asking questions empowers people, especially adults. Giving readymade solutions to adults reduces their thinking ability and increases their dependence on others. So, ask questions instead of giving answers... that way people will take ownership of the solutions they have generated.'

And we agree completely with Mr. Gothi. In our several years of experience in Training and Coaching top managers and business owners, only those solutions have ever got implemented where the trainee felt 'ownership' for the solution.

In our one-to-one meeting with Mr. Agarwal, we unearthed several causes for the delay in outstanding collections through intense probing and appreciative enquiry. While, Mr. Agarwal waited for the answers to come from us, all we offered him were questions... questions that rattled him and challenged several of the beliefs he had held dearly. We found out that it had become a standard practice with Mr. Agarwal not to speak of any credit terms while selling to the retailers. All the discussions revolved around order size, cloth designs, delivery time and material quality. The distributor avoided the conversation on credit terms for fear of losing order and the retailer was too happy the subject not being discussed at all.

After the material was despatched, there were no follow-up calls or reminders from Mr. Agarwal's team. Mr. Agarwal was not in the habit of conducting structured reviews with his team either. So the issue of outstanding collections would only crop up if the parent company, AVN Textiles pressurized him for payments. He would then sit with his team and review the list of retailers who had crossed the sixty days deadline. He would then ask his team to follow up with the small retailers on the telephone whereas he himself would follow-up with the wholesalers and large retailers. It's anybody's guess that by this time, 80-90 days would have elapsed from the date of despatch.

"When the first reminder for payment is sent after 80 days, how's one supposed to collect money within 60 days, Mr. Agarwal?" Mr. Agarwal had no answer to this question, but agreed that something had been going wrong. On further probing, we realized that even these follow-up calls were made half-heartedly and under the constant fear that the retailer would take offence.

After a gruelling two-hour session, Mr. Agarwal agreed to work on a few things. He decided to have a weekly review meeting with his team to identify in advance the retailers who might cross the sixty days deadline. He decided to ensure that the first follow-up call was made within a week of the despatch. He and his team agreed to make 'follow-up for collections' a regular and structured process. That meant the first follow-up call happened within a week, the second after 15 days, the third after 30 days and the fourth call on or before the 45th day. These were supposed to be polite requests, but at the same time firm, phone-calls to retailers reminding them of the outstanding amount and the corresponding due dates.

He recruited a customer service executive to visit retailers who had crossed 45 days. This person's job was to work closely with the retailers and enable them to pay on time through better merchandising and enhanced counter sales.

A major decision that Mr. Agarwal took for himself was not to indulge in 'dumping'. He decided to look at the retailer as his business partner and focus primarily on enhancing retailers' sales, rather than his personal sales. He decided to identify the retailers' needs through probing and provide only what was required by them. Although he had a fear that it might impact his sales figures, he was pretty sure of his decision as he felt it was the right approach. To cover up for any loss that might arise out of this decision, he decided to meet up with new retailers who might do good business with him. We suggested that he read a book to enhance his probing skills and then practice what he learned in the market. Surprisingly, Mr. Agarwal picked up the suggestion and expressed his desire to read something on the subject. We suggested Neil Rackham's 'SPIN Selling' to him, which is an excellent book on the subject of probing (a must-read for every sales professional, business-owner and top manager).

A year later, when Mr. Agarwal came for this year's Distributor Meet, he shared a different story with the audience. His outstanding dues have come down tremendously, from an average of six months to 75 days now. Most of his retailers pay before sixty days. There are still a few big retailers who pay after 75-80 days of despatch. However, "they have improved from paying in 180 days to paying in 80 days… and I'm quite happy with that improvement," says Mr. Agarwal. He said, "Initially there was a lot of resistance from retailers. Some even threatened to stop doing business with us. But, we persisted in a friendly and courteous manner. We shifted our focus from selling to them to selling through them." That definitely helped. Out of the 250 retailers, three quit while a few others reduced their business with us. The business dropped in the first few weeks. But we were fearless, because we were appointing new retailers in these areas. In fact these new retailers understood us better than our older ones.

Thus the overall impact on sales was positive. We sold around ₹15 crores of material last year. But, because the realization of money has become faster, our profits have gone up significantly. We have more cash now to experiment with new marketing ideas and to give better service to our customers, i.e. retailers. I think the biggest achievement is that most retailers have started viewing me as their business partner rather than merely a sales person with the sole aim of dumping goods. That is an invaluable feeling to live with!"

FACING THIS TRUTH RIGHT NOW

All of us have challenges pertaining to our job and our goals. Some of us are waiting for the promotion that is long due, some of us are waiting to crack a big order, some of us are waiting for the right people to join our organizations while some of us are waiting for the love of our life.

While many of us would like to believe that the fault is in the others, the truth is something else. The truth is that our big order has still not happened because there's something we don't know about big-order-closing, we haven't got the promotion to the next post because we are missing on certain key skills required for that position, we haven't got the best people to join our teams because there's something we don't know about attracting the best talent, the love of our life hasn't become ours because there's something about his or her needs that we haven't decoded yet...so on and so forth! The list is endless.

There are so many achievements yet to happen in our life because of our current knowledge, skills and expertise in those matters or the lack of it. It is therefore imperative to find out 'what is it that I don't know?' about these matters that is preventing me in going to the next level. The more we keep saying 'I know everything,' the farther we move away from goal-accomplishment.

In his path-breaking book *The Alchemist*, Paulo Coelho writes – *Alchemy exists so that everyone will search for his treasure, find it, and then want to be better than he was in his former life. Lead (the metal) will play its role until the world has no further need for lead; and then lead will have to turn itself into gold. That's what alchemists do. They show that, when we strive to become better than we are, everything around us becomes better too.*

- Would you like to have a turnaround like Mr. Agarwal for all your goals?
- Would you like to see yourselves achieving what you have planned to achieve?
- Would you like to develop the competence to take up the next level challenge?
- Would you like to feel powerful RIGHT NOW?

LIVING THE TRUTH RIGHT NOW

Write at least three goals that you have been wanting to achieve. These may be from your personal or professional life. Doesn't matter what the goals are! But, they have to be important to you.

An important goal for you might be 'I want to become a Sales Manager in two years', 'I want to become the Production Head in three years', 'I want to take my mother-father on a world trip in the next five years', 'I want this client to give me his 50 percent business within a year', 'I want my son to look up to me as an ideal mother', 'I want my company to be listed on the Bombay Stock Exchange in five years' or 'I want to run five kms a day' and so on and so forth.

Write these three goals on the next page. Remember your goal must be SMART (Specific, Measurable, Attainable, Realistic and Time-bound). Say you write, 'I want to grow in my career.' A smarter goal would be, 'I want to be the GM-Operations within three years.' Or you might write, 'I want to enhance my business turnover.' A smarter goal would be 'I want to increase my sales turnover from ₹5 crores this year to ₹7 crores in the next financial year.'

Now please describe why this goal is important to you. What is it that might happen once you achieve this goal? What rewards or opportunities you might get because of accomplishing this goal?

Writing why these goals are important will give you clarity regarding the motivation behind your goals. Goals per se are not motivating by themselves. It is what happens to us and our lives because of these goals that are truly motivating.

Goal 1 ....

Why This Goal Is So Important To Me? ....

....

....

....

....

Goal 2 ....

Why This Goal Is So Important To Me? ....

....

....

....

....

Goal 3 ....

Why This Goal Is So Important To Me? ....

....

....

....

....

LIVING THE TRUTH RIGHT NOW

On the next page is the key to living this truth right now. Write down your goal and its importance in the first column. Now identify what skills or competencies you might require to achieve that goal. Make a list of all the competencies you might require, don't leave out any. To know what competencies might be required you may talk to people who have accomplished that task before. Say you want to know what competencies you might require to get your company listed on the stock exchange. Then you can have a chat with your friend who has recently listed his company. Say you want to become the manager of your department; you can talk to your current departmental manager to list out the skill sets required. In the next column, write your current competencies and skill-sets. You can easily get to know your current skill sets by looking at all those things that you are doing well or are generally good at. A quick comparison of the second and third column will give us our fourth column 'the gap areas'. Now, this is the column we need to focus on. Finally, in the row below, please make an action plan on how you will fill this 'gap area'. Remember, if we stay the way we are, we will stay where we are. So write anything and everything that you can do to overcome this gap area. And again, this action plan must be a SMART action plan. Let's do it right away.

MY ACTION PLAN

My Goal & its Importance	Competencies/ Skill Sets Required	My Current Skill Set	The Gap Areas

1. The Books I Will Read–

2. The Training Workshops I Will Attend–

3. The People I Will Seek Guidance From–

My Goal & its Importance	Competencies/ Skill Sets Required	My Current Skill Set	The Gap Areas

1. The Books I Will Read:

2. The Training Workshops I Will Attend:

3. The People I Will Seek Guidance From:

My Goal & Its Importance	Competencies/ Skill Sets Required	My Current Skill Set	The Gap Areas

1. The Books I Will Read:

2. The Training Workshops I Will Attend:

3. The People I Will Seek Guidance From:

3

Your Truth

3

My Emotions and Actions are Controlled by People around Me.

I am very sensitive…
I get very angry because people anger me….
My wife upset me terribly so I refuse to go to work today….
My husband is very insensitive and this hurts me….
I could be anything I wanted to, but people around me don't allow
*   me to….*
I am so demotivated because of the way life has treated me….
I cry very easily, and people know this and they misuse it…
My boss makes me very angry, so I take all kinds of wrong decisions..
I always wake up wanting to do a lot of good things…but people
*   really upset me – my wife, my mother, my boss, the taxi driver….*
I could have done so much, if only people would stop playing with
*   my emotions…*

If the above is you, welcome to the 'My-life-is-not-my-own' Club.
There are millions of members in this club too. They are the ones
who are always ready to cry, whine, complain and gripe. They can
be made to laugh easily and made to cry even more easily. They are
emotional and emotionally dependent on people for every activity
and decision in life. They are of the absolute opinion that people
around them are in a conspiracy to anger them and upset them.

It is difficult to speak to them, because they misunderstand
everything. They are always trying to find non-existent 'meanings'
in what people say. And all they come up with are very demotivating
interpretations. They always complain that no one understands

them. They cry at the smallest provocation. They are emotionally dependent on others all the time. And they make their own life very miserable.

Are you one of the members?

What's Your Story?
Below this paragraph, you will find a table that is designed to enable you to face Your Truth.

Step 1
The Belief – Pick out one or similar sentences from the previous page that you utter or think regularly.

Step 2
The Evidence – Write down at least one instance of why those sentences have been repeated by you so often.

Step 3
The Outcome – Write your feelings when you have 'proved' that the sentences are your life's Truth.

The Belief ……..	The Evidence ……..

The Outcome ………

Step 4
Read on…

THE STORY OF AVARAM BARON

Avaram Baron was a very successful business owner. He owned a huge family business of construction right in the heart of Germany. His great grandfather had started the business and his family was one of the most influential people in the city of Hamburg He was well educated and had several successful projects across the country. He was often invited to speak at business schools and seminars on entrepreneurship and was an author of several books. His diary was always filled with social engagements and there was seldom an evening when him and his lovely wife were not entertaining some of the top ministers and industry leaders in their beautiful home.

He had everything going for him. A luxurious city house, a country mansion, several offices across the country, enough money to live a life of extravagance, a beautiful wife, a loving brother and two very proud parents.

The period was 1939 and Adolf Hitler had begun persecuting Jews in the country. His aim was to eradicate Jews from the face of the earth. His meteoric rise to power and desire for Europe's domination which he began by invading Poland led to World War II.

Avaram Baron was a Jew.

Like Avaram, the Jews in Germany were a hard-working, ambitious lot. And it came as a shock and a surprise to Avaram and his family when they heard about the atrocities being committed on their fellow Jews. But knowing that he had tremendous influence with the policy makers of the city, the Baron family was not too worried about their own situation. They were rich enough and influential enough and German enough, they argued. What happened next was a shock to them!

One day, the Baron family was having their evening meal, when a platoon of soldiers barged in. They dragged them from the dinner table to the nearest police station and tortured them till they accepted that they were part of a conspiracy against the führer. They were then made to sign declarations to that effect and their property was confiscated under the pretext of national security.

Avaram was then dragged with his family to the railway station and they were stuffed into trains that were on their way to the dreaded concentration camps. There were thousands of Jews who were being meted out the same treatment. And it was with anxiety and despair that the Baron family saw the last of their home and their city.

I assume that you know the size of a compartment of a goods train. The Germans stuffed the Jew prisoners, 150 to a compartment – with no place to sit, no place to stand and no air to breathe. There was no provision for food, water or even a toilet. And it was under these sub-human conditions that Avaram saw and experienced a life that would make your flesh crawl and change your very perception of life.

The journey in the train took 7 days to complete before it reached its destination. And during its course, it did not stop even once. The temperature was sub-zero and there was no air to breathe for those who were not near the air holes punched into the walls. Several people died due to severe lack of oxygen in that crowded train and Avaram himself had to travel next to the dead body of a young boy who died because he was unable to breathe in the overcrowded space.

When the train ground to a halt on the seventh day and the doors were opened, there was hardly anyone who had the strength to crawl out. The ones who didn't tumble out were left

for dead on the railway tracks to be preyed upon by vultures
and dogs. The ones who survived, Avaram amongst them,
were then marched to the station, where they were divided
into two groups. The young men in one and the older men
in the other. A concerned Avaram, who had lost track of his
family, asked one of his mates, "My parents may be in that
lot. Hope the soldiers will be kind to them. Where are the
older people being taken?" The man looked at him strangely
and pointed out to some factories in the distance, which had
evil smelling smoke pouring out of its chimneys, "They are
being taken there." A worried Avaram asked him, "Hope they
won't make them work too hard. They are old and suffer from
arthritis." The man softly replied, "They are not being taken
there to work. That smell may be them."

I am sure you have heard of the infamous gas chambers.
The gas chambers were a simple way to get rid of people who
would be unable to work for the Germans. The chambers were
essentially huge metal ovens in which people would be herded,
naked and locked in. A toxic gas would then be introduced
into these chambers through pipes running across the ceiling
until the people inside died of asphyxiation, screaming in
terror. The bodies (some of them miraculously alive) would
then be burnt in the chamber itself by turning on the heat
knobs. These ovens which were used for smelting iron and
steel became the graveyards for lakhs of old Jews, whose only
aspiration might have been to live the end of their lives in
relative peace with their loving children and grandchildren.

Avaram, with other Jewish prisoners, was then herded
towards the dreaded concentration camps. It was a three-day
march in minus 20 degrees temperature. The concentration
camp was a large piece of land, surrounded by barbed and
electrified fences, which were continuously manned by

soldiers. This enclosed land had the prisons and the living quarters of the soldiers and officers. The prisons were huge windowless barracks which had three-tier bunker beds, each bed crammed with 4-5 prisoners in the space of one. The floors were covered with filth and humans, each merging into the other so seamlessly that one was indistinguishable from the other. And these were the same men who, until a few days back, would often lose their own way in the multitude of rooms that they had in their vast homes.

Avaram, later recollects that once your senses were numbed to the dirt, stink, filth and cold, life in the camp was almost simple, compared to the complexities of 'real' life. In 'real' life you had to take decisions – what to wear to a party ("The red velvet or the blue satin, sweetheart?"), what to have for lunch ("Baked or roasted, darling?"), where to go for dinner ("I think we should go across to the club tonight, honey, or do you prefer to go across to the Savoy?"), where to invest ("I believe that the property to the east of the city centre is a great bet, old man."), what to gift ("Should I buy her the diamond bracelet or should I buy her a car for her birthday?"), where to holiday ("We went to Switzerland last year, we were planning for the Far East this May").

'Real' life was a life filled with intense thought of the future. And now in this hell-hole, for all the prisoners, their burning ambition, desires, vision, goals had reduced to one common need – food.

The routine at the camp was iron-clad. There was a bugle at 6 am. The prisoners had to assemble in line for the head count. They were then served their only meal for the day – a bowl of soup. If you were lucky, you would find a few pieces of cabbage or a couple of green peas in your bowl. The later you came in the line, the possibility of getting sediments was high.

But it came with a risk. If you were too late, there might not be any left.

Avaram and the other prisoners, their stomachs growling with hunger, would constantly recollect the spreads that they would have at home, as they gulped down their meagre fare. Their mouths salivated and their hearts contracted when they recollected the amount of food they had wasted in their previous life. The huge mounds of herbed rice, hot bread, mountains of creamed potatoes, rich gravy swimming in butter, roasted meat glazed with honey, the thick stews with enough vegetables and meat in the bowl to serve a roomful of prisoners...and oh! The desserts! Chocolate-covered pastries, cream-filled custards, meringue-stuffed eclairs, syrupy puddings, sweetened fruits, roasted almonds wrapped in dates and coated with pistachios. Big, grown, strong men who had never shed a tear at the death of a relative, now cried copious tears at the thought of food, as they secretly crammed fistfuls of dirty snow into their mouth to ward off the intense pain of hunger.

They all promised themselves and each other, that once they were released from the prison in a few days, (of course they would be released. They were decent law-abiding citizens of a country they loved. And the world at large would not allow these atrocities to be committed on innocent people, right?), they would go home and never waste food ever again. They shared recipes and descriptions of food... the pastry in the corner bakery, the special potatoes that a mother made, the stuffed meat that a sister made... and they all invited each other home... the moment they were released from the prison in a few days (of course they would be released...). And the discussion would continue in anxious brave whispers throughout the night.

Once breakfast was done, they would be marched across the snow to their place of work. The work allotted would depend on the plan for the week – clear the snow here, flatten a road there, carry loads of provisions from one place to the other, lay railway tracks for the soldiers and trains, clear the camp, sweep the soldiers' quarters or clean the ever-increasing mound of human waste around the camp. The work was physical, mindless, exhausting and degrading. There was hardly any break throughout the day and only the fittest survived the cold and the labour.

In the beginning, the prisoners tried to ingratiate themselves to the soldiers, believing that people were generally nice – including soldiers. They truly believed that one human could simply not commit such atrocities on the other. They were naïve enough to believe that if you were nice to someone, they would in turn be nice to you. The soldiers reserved their worst treatments for these prisoners – the 'nice' ones. They were subjected to inhuman atrocities and there was often a day when a dozen prisoners did not return from their visits to the soldiers' quarters and were never seen again.

In the first few days, hopes ran high. With every boom or rattle, they would silently cheer, convinced that the American troops were arriving to free them. They would look at each other with shining eyes. They awaited their moment of freedom and whispered to each other 'Don't forget. First stop is my house on the way back to yours. My mother is going to dish out the world's best food in a matter of minutes.' And they waited. And waited.

Conviction turned to Hope. Hope turned to Anxiety. Anxiety to Disbelief. Disbelief to Anger. And finally Anger to Hopelessness. They say that a man who has hope can survive the most fatal of illnesses and the most terrible of circumstances. And a man who has lost hope finds even daily survival impossible. And that's exactly how the prisoners reacted to their condition. For a while they waited for the soldiers to treat them more humanely. Then they waited to be rescued by American troops. Then they waited for God to strike the cruel soldiers dead. And then they just waited for death.

Thousands lost their will to live when they faced the reality that there was no rescue. The hopelessness of their situation sucked the very life out of them. And then the avalanche of suicides started.

There were three ways in which the prisoners started committing suicide.

The first method was the most torturous, and took a lot of will-power. It was to stop eating. Not touch the bowl of soup given to one at the beginning of the day. Not to cram snow into the mouth like others did. The same snow that kept people from getting dehydrated. Passing on the bowl of soup to the person next to him was perhaps the hardest thing for a prisoner to do, when his own stomach was twisting with hunger.

There were many who would wait for the person next to them to try this method of suicide, so that they could grab the bowl before someone else did. It was seldom that one tried to dissuade the other from suicide. The food was too precious. And then the doomed prisoner would wait for the cramps to start. It started as a small twinge and within 24 hours, the prisoner would be rolling on the ground clutching his abdomen writhing on the floor in his own filth in excruciating agony before he died due to extreme dehydration.

The second method was easier but took a lot of courage. It was to stop working. Right in the middle of the work day, *the prisoner would just stop working. The soldiers would see him standing there motionless and attack him with their fists, shoes and butts of their heavy guns. If he could be brave enough for about 5 to 7 minutes, they would eventually get tired and shoot him dead.*

The third method was the easiest, but also the most risky. Here, the prisoner would sneak out of his barracks at night and would run into the barbed wire fence. Hundreds of volts of electricity would ravage his body and render him dead within a minute.

But if a soldier ever caught a prisoner trying to sneak out in this manner, his life would become hell. Because the punishment for this was to hang the prisoner upside down from a tree and torture him for the next several days to set an example to all the others. The torture would vary from making him eat his own filth to pouring red ants over his raw wounds, from a punch to his head to a bayonet through it. The prisoner would beg for mercy and death, while the soldiers gleefully laid bets on how long the prisoner would live. There were parties and prizes for the platoon leaders who reported the most number of deaths by suicide.

And as though this was not enough, the dead bodies were thrown into deep pits that had been dug up earlier. Some of them as deep and wide as 40 feet x 40 feet x 40 feet. The bodies would keep piling till there was no room for others before the pit was allowed to be closed. And then the next pit would start to be filled. The stench seeped not only into the skin but the very souls of the prisoners. The intention was to break the spirit of these Jewish prisoners and it did.

Of all the prisoners who passed through that concentration camp, only three survived from the first batch. They were eventually released by the invading American troops in

1943 after having spent four long years in that camp. One of them died on the way to the hospital. The second survivor committed suicide within a month, being unable to cope up with the real world, haunted by nightmares that terrorized him and drove him to insanity. And the third man to survive was Avaram Baron.

He was interviewed several weeks later and these are excerpts from his interview:

Reporter: Don't you hate the German soldiers for the treatment that they meted out to you?

Avaram: No, not really. I guess they were just doing their job. Just as I was doing mine. Their job was to ensure that we died. My job was to ensure that I survived. Their daily target was the number of people who should have died at their hands at the end of the day. My daily target was to survive the day and prepare to face the next. I promised myself that I will get out of that place alive, find my family and friends who may have survived, restart my business, make lots of money again, create value for people, make a difference to people's lives, dance again, read again, live again. I guess my targets were stronger than theirs.

Reporter: What made you survive when so many others couldn't?

Avaram: I told myself daily a thousand times that I have greater things to achieve in life. If I allowed the German soldiers to take control of my life, then I'd never survive and never fulfil all my dreams. I realized that you cannot make people do what you want them to do. People have control over

> *their thoughts and actions, just as only you have control over yours. And I was not going to give anyone the right to upset me to the extent that I sacrifice my dreams, my ambition, my future, my life. Because you see, I truly believe that no one can upset me without my permission. And that my life control belongs to me.* Like I was saying, People have control over their thoughts and actions, just as you have control over yours.

THE STORY OF AVARAM BARON – DECODED

The story of Avaram is inspired by a real story (with literary freedom of course), the life-story of Dr. Viktor Frankl, who has written a book titled *Man's Search for Meaning*. The book narrates his experiences of concentration camps and the life inside them. It has brought tears to people's eyes. They simply couldn't imagine how someone can keep himself motivated to overcome such excruciatingly painful circumstances.

But his pain is not too different from the pain of people who face 'difficult' people around them every day. We can only imagine the frustration, the demotivation, the loss of confidence that such people face on a day to day basis.

What Avaram said in his interview were the words of a truly great man. A man who decided that one needs to feel passionately enough about one's own goals in life. One has to visualize a better life and a better future and not allow others to get in the way between one and one's goals in life.

Our problem is that we allow too many people to control our lives. We literally hand over our life remote control to them. We laugh when they press the laugh button. We cry when they press the cry button. We get anxious when they press the stress button.

I know of hundreds of people whose every action and emotion is dependent on the people around them. They never live their own lives on their own terms. And the biggest surprise – many of them are super achievers. They have done so much in life. And yet, they allow their wives, their husbands, their bosses, their subordinates, their children to literally rule their life.

We love the way, Tapasya (Vijaya's eight-year-old daughter) handled a situation, where she used this truth. She was playing on the swing, when an eleven year old boy walked up to her and said, "Go and play elsewhere because I don't like to see you in this part of the garden." She replied, "Why should I do what you want me to do? If you don't like to see me play here, why don't you go and play elsewhere? I refuse to go anywhere else." When she was narrating this incident in the evening to Vijaya, she explained, "You had told me that "My life remote control belongs to me". Why should I allow that boy to control my actions?' Love ya, girl!

BREAK FREE TRUTH 3 –

My life 'remote control' belongs to me

BREAK FREE TRUTH 3 – IN A 'KICK-ASS' FORMAT

Hmm! So you are back, eager to know how you can be in control of your own life? What can we say, except 'Stop Whining'. People can be sensitive to our so-called pain only for some time. After that they get irritated, which makes many of us irritating people to know. That's not very inspiring. Is it?

What makes these people so sensitive to others… many reasons combined into one! All of them are discussed in detail in the chapter *Facing The Truth Right Now*. However, one definite reason for their sensitivity is a false sense of self, a self-image that doesn't gel with reality, in simple terms their ego is a bit bigger than what their achievements can boast of.

Yeah! You heard that right! EGO – if you are one of the members of this club, then that's what you probably hide behind your so-called 'sensitivity'. And the mismatch between ego and achievements gives birth to the 'victim mentality'. 'My husband should be nice to me' – Why? Why should your husband be nice to you? Are you Aishwarya Rai? "Everyone should be kind to me" – Why? Why should everyone be kind to you? Who are you… Mother Teresa reborn? "My boss should be appreciative of me" – Why? Why should your boss be appreciative of you? You have just won the *Manager of The Year* Award for the tenth time in a row?

If you are a member of this club, please wake up to the fact that expecting people to be 'nice', 'kind', 'sweet', 'understanding' to you is 'EGO' inflated a thousand times. Yes! Even more than those of the 'I-prefer-to-stay-the-way-I-am' guys in Truth No. 2.

The only person from whom you can demand any understanding is YOU. When you choose not to be nice to yourself, why should someone else bother? When you don't consider yourself important enough, why should someone else? When you don't respect yourself, why should someone else? And you will cover it all up by saying that I sacrifice because my happiness lies in the happiness of others – my family, my children, my husband, my wife, my colleagues, my subordinates. So, if that is your decision – *then be happy, don't complain!*

We are going to take the liberty of a narrating a conversation between 'W' and 'C', where 'W' stands for 'Whiner', 'C' stands for 'Controller', and 'P' for 'Controlling Person 2' (Not Woman, Child and *Pati* (Husband), like you might have presumed).

SCENE – A middle class home on a Saturday. Living room. Time around 12.30 pm. Husband reading the paper and sipping tea. Son watching TV and playing a video game on his phone. Both of them munching a plate full of snacks. Mother enters the room and slips her feet into a pair of sandals.

C – *Mom, where are you going?*

W – *Just to Vijaya Aunty's house. Thought I will catch up with her. Haven't met her for the past several months and I wanted to share some things that have been troubling me.*

C – *But who will serve me my food?*

W – *Oh? I thought you just said that you weren't hungry. And anyway, you have been munching something or the other since morning.*

C – *I am not hungry now. But I will be in 15 minutes.*

W – *The food is ready. You just have to serve yourself.*

C – *I can't serve myself. You wait and serve me and then go.*

W – *Ok. Can I just keep the plate ready? You can just pick it up from the kitchen.*

C – NO! I want hot food.

W – It is very hot. In 15 minutes it will not cool down. You anyway don't like hot food.

C – Today I want to eat hot food. So, you don't go anywhere.

W to P – Can you serve him food? I will be back in half an hour.

P – Arre, yaar! Saturday is the only day I get to relax. You meet your friend in the evening.

W – But you said your friends will be here for dinner.

P – Yes. So, go on some other day.

W – I promised her last week, too. But last week your parents were here for lunch and dinner.

P – Oho! So, your kitty party is more important than my friends and family?

W – I didn't say that. Ok. I will just call Vijaya aunty up and tell her that I can't meet her today.

Later on the phone, W, pours her heart out to Vijaya Aunty–

V – Arre! Why didn't you come today? I waited for you.

W – What to do, Vijaya? My husband doesn't respect me. And my son is so stubborn. No one listens to me. No one cares about me. No one loves me. (weeping)

Sweetheart, first YOU respect yourself. YOU listen to yourself. YOU care about you. YOU love yourself. The world will follow. (And stop crying for God's sake).

So, go to the next page. The Tracker awaits you. All the best.

THE 5 BREAK FREE TRUTHS TRACKER - WEEK 3

Your Truth - My emotions and actions are controlled by people around me

The Truth - My life 'remote control' belongs to me

What I Believed – My Truth	I am (was, until now) very sure that my life simply did not belong to me. I was so sensitive that people around me were deciding what my mood would be today. My happiness would be because my wife was happy. My sadness would be because my mother is unhappy.
What The Truth Is – My Realizations	As I read the story of Avaram Baron, I realized that people can only upset me if I allow them. No one can upset me if I make up my mind to remain unruffled. People don't control my emotions, I do.
My Next Step	I intend to repeat to myself that no one can upset me and that my life remote belongs to me, at least 20 times in the morning before I leave home. I am going to remember all the great things that have happened to me at the end of the day, so that I wake up motivated the next day.
My Truth Partner	Ronak Shah (Boss)

THE 5 BREAK FREE TRUTHS TRACKER - WEEK 3

Your Truth - My emotions and actions are controlled by people around me

The Truth - My life 'remote control' belongs to me

What I Believed – My Truth	

What The Truth Is – My Realizations	
My Next Step	
My Truth Partner	

HOW OTHERS AROUND YOU DISCOVERED THIS TRUTH

In his classic book *Games People Play*, Dr. Eric Berne maintains that people play games to achieve ulterior motives. His theory on *games* is extremely helpful in understanding people and the motives behind their actions. While explaining a game 'If it weren't for you', Dr. Berne has given a very beautiful, yet a hard-hitting example. It goes like this –

Mrs. White complained that her husband severely restricted her social activities, so that she had never learned to dance. Due to changes in her attitude brought about by psychiatric treatment, her husband became less sure of himself and more indulgent. Mrs. White was then free to enlarge the scope of her activities. She signed up for dancing classes, and then discovered to her despair that she had a morbid fear of dance floors and had to abandon this project. This unfortunate adventure laid bare some important aspects of the structure of her marriage. Out of her many suitors, she had picked a domineering man for a husband. She was then in a position to complain that she could do all sorts of things 'if it weren't for you'. Many of her women friends also had domineering husbands and when they met for their morning coffee, they spent a good deal of time playing 'If it weren't for him....!'

Haven't we come across hundreds and thousands of game players? They are the ones who truly believe that their life's remote control is in someone else's hands. Their statements either start or end with 'because of my husband...' or 'because of my wife' or 'because of my father' or 'because of my boss'... well the list is as long as the number of people in their lives.

Two years ago, Sarfaraz Hussain came face to face with this truth during a performance review facilitated by Liberation Coaches. Sarfaraz is a sales manager with United Constructions Ltd. (UCL), a specialist in mid-sized residential apartments and had construction projects in various cities running simultaneously. Their buyers mostly belonged to the rich and super-rich class of society. They had hired our consultancy services for Organization Development that comprised of defining the key result areas of all the employees right from the CEO to the frontline executives, conducting monthly performance reviews and facilitating training programs for the entire sales team. As an organization, UCL was a good place to work for anyone who was a performer. But, life was tough for those who couldn't deliver as UCL placed a lot of premium on the achievement of results. 'Beg, borrow, steal... I don't care! Bring me results!' said the CEO, Mr. Anand Vaidyanathan, himself a fiery leader with a formidable track record.

Sarfaraz had joined UCL just about a year ago. This

was his second job; his first experience was with Lakshmi Constructions, a company that was much smaller and had only one or two projects running on the outskirts of the city. This company designed apartments aimed at the middle and lower middle class. Sarfaraz was extremely happy when he took up the UCL offer last year. The salary package was good; the incentives were much better, the team here was much bigger and professional, but most importantly UCL was a renowned brand to work with.

Sarfaraz wasn't exactly a sales super-star in his past job. But, he wasn't bad either. At Lakshmi, he was part of a small team of three sales executives who reported directly to the managing director of the company. During his days in Lakshmi Constructions, there were times when days and weeks would go by without a single apartment being sold. Prospective buyers would come, take a site tour, ask a lot of questions and leave, never to return back. Back then, he used to face lots of objections (a term used to denote buyer concerns) from the customers. 'Your rates are pretty high', 'the other builder is giving a discount', 'what is the guarantee you will deliver on time?', 'never heard the name of this builder, is this your first project?' and so on and so forth. Those were painful days and he always used to wonder how life would be for the big brands in real estate. 'Those guys don't bargain' his colleagues told him, 'you know, they sell on their terms. Take it or leave it. That's what they say! They don't sell, buyers form queues outside their offices! It's a different story for them dude, not like us!'

And then, UCL happened. Sarfaraz couldn't have been happier. He had been waiting to be part of a large organization where the brand name would work. He had been waiting for the day when buyers would form a queue outside his office and he would say "take it or leave it" and before the buyer could react, he had dreamt of calling out to the next guy in line... Next! His first few months were pretty good as the company had recently launched a new marketing campaign. The number of enquiries and walk-ins (prospective buyers actually visiting the site) surged and nearly every sales person achieved his/her target. Your conversion ratio (the percentage of deals closed out of total number of walk-ins handled) didn't matter as the numbers were large and someone or the other came with a cheque for a down payment. That kept the cash bell ringing and the GM – Sales, Jehangir Nagpurwalla happy. Sarfaraz looked up to Jehangir and wanted to become like him. Everyone was an achiever then. But, those were the days when Sarfaraz had recently joined.

As the impact of the marketing campaign died and number of walk-ins came down, every enquiry became valuable and every walk-in worth its weight in gold. In just a few months, the team became a medley of a few who achieved their targets month after month and a majority that was struggling to even achieve what can be called average sales. Sarfaraz got tagged as the below average salesperson. Jehangir was unhappy with him and spared no opportunity to show it as well. Jehangir had risen from the ranks and had been a sales super-star himself, so his tolerance for weak salesmen was obviously low. Sarfaraz saw his world falling apart. He was thoroughly demotivated.

Lack of enough number of walk-ins meant reduced number of deals and lower sales. Lower sales meant an unhappy boss who was ever-ready to compare your figures with that of other salesmen. That only led to lower confidence and a state of demotivation. A demotivated salesman inevitably has a lower conversion ratio. It was a vicious cycle Sarfaraz was caught in.

"I get demotivated when people are not impressed by my sales presentation. You know I work so hard to give impressive sales pitches. I was even selected as the 'Best Speaker' in my MBA days. Here, it's a different story. Customers are too well informed and have become too shrewd to handle. They know exactly which builder is offering what rates and what discounts. That's very disconcerting! When one sales meeting is unproductive, it affects my rest of the sales meetings for the day. Those who pay attention to my presentations are not even worthy of buying our apartments. And the problem is I get more of them! I was told to classify prospects as A, B and C – A being the most prosperous with the ability to buy our apartments whereas the B ones having the less prosperity and the C ones having the least. There is no point paying too much attention to the B and the C categories, while the number of A category prospects is so low and they don't seem to understand me. We don't follow up with prospects or meet up with them anywhere other than our sales office… we don't want to show them we are desperate… after all, we are UCL."

Sarfaraz was opening his heart. He continued, "I'm now afraid of Jehangir. I have always wanted so much to impress him and to make him happy. However, every time he calls me in, I know I'm in for a critical feedback session. I thought at least he will understand me. Every word he says is so depressing. It upsets me completely. But, the bloody problem is he's right too! On one hand he passes on several enquiries to other salespeople and on the other I myself don't feel like handling newer enquiries. What if I screw them up? I do not like myself nowadays and I don't think anybody likes me here either."

One-to-one reviews with Sarfaraz by our reviewer opened up a whole new world for him. Part of his challenge was because of deficiency of skills in sales. For example, he had placed too much stress on 'presentation' rather than on need analysis. He was sharing all his reasons for selling the apartments but was not identifying the buyers' reasons for buying the apartments. He and the entire team relied only on the enquiries generated through the marketing drives. However, there was no initiative by the sales team to generate enquiries from their own sources like friends, family and the most important source of them all – people who had already bought apartments at UCL township. Sarfaraz had focused too much on categorization of prospects, while he had no tools or valid data to categorize them in such a manner. Most of the categorization was based on pure assumptions, like the prospect's dressing style, his/her communication (can't speak English, must be a 'C' category prospect!) or the kinds of accessories he or she used! Even the Customer Information Form that was filled by the prospects gave only a basic idea about the prospect's current status (your profession, your age, your annual income, the required size of your apartment etc.) and no idea about why he wanted to buy a UCL apartment. Although pretty unintentional, it appeared as if there was an attempt by the entire team to disqualify a large number of prospects as B and C, thus making them unqualified prospects. This obviously improved their conversion ratio as the number of deals were compared with the number of 'qualified prospects' and not with the total number of telephonic enquiries and walk-ins.

However, the major part of his challenge stemmed from the fact that he had repeated a lie often enough – 'my emotions and actions are controlled by people around me.' Unless this lie was uncovered and Sarfaraz was made to face the truth, there was no point in developing the skill areas. Statements like 'I get demotivated when people are not impressed,' or 'when one sales meeting is unproductive, it affects my rest of the sales meetings for the day' or 'we don't want to show them we are desperate' or 'I have always wanted so much to impress him' and 'I do not like myself nowadays and I don't think anybody likes me here either' only underlined this lie. It took several one-to-one meetings with Sarfaraz to make him realize the he had given his life's 'remote control' in other people's hands. He was allowing people to press the buttons they liked and he was only responding to the commands. His motivation depended solely on customers liking his presentations or on Jehangir saying 'Good job!' and both these things never happened!

As Sarfaraz slowly started to realize this, he began looking at things differently. We coached him to look at every rejection by a prospect as a part of life. No sales person has ever become great without being rejected by customers, no actors have made it big time without being rejected by several directors, no politician has ever become successful without being rejected by the very people he served, no singer has ever achieved greatness without being rejected by his or her fans and no author has ever written a bestseller that was not rejected by at least half a dozen publishers as 'bullshit'. None of the great minds had it easy with people around them. People were tough with them, hard on them, critical of them and made life difficult for them with their words and actions. However, people who achieved greatness looked at every rejection as an opportunity to improve.

We brought to Sarfaraz's notice that he had a choice every time he was faced with a rejection – either get demotivated and stay that way or to identify where he fell short, mend his approach and bounce back with renewed vigour to face the next sales meeting. As one of our decade-old client (who is also a dear friend now) Mr. Deepak Dhabalia says, "My initial years in insurance sales were harrowing. I could only see people rejecting me and the solutions I was offering.

It was very demotivating. Things started changing when I changed my attitude towards rejections. When I looked at every rejection not as a hurdle, but as another chapter in the Science of Sales; life changed completely for me! I was able to stay focused and motivated most of the time and the valuable learning from all those rejections added to my vast repertoire of knowledge. Rejections kept teaching me what not to do on a daily basis and find out the 'why' behind a client's decision to buy or not buy. Today most of my clients are high networth individuals or A category clients as we call them. I don't sell insurance anymore, I only build relations… sales is what automatically happens." Mr. Dhabalia is invited today to speak at several seminars to speak of his experiences with rejections.

As Sarfaraz started taking control of his emotions, he learnt to look at customers in a different way. "Customer is God. He is not an interruption to our business. Rather, he is the only reason why we started it" said Mahatma Gandhi. Sarfaraz realized it was a folly to expect customers to stand in a queue and thus he was able to challenge the big brand mentality he had fallen prey to. He began questioning his own approach of not following up with prospects or not meeting them at places of their choice like their offices or residences. Here we needed a lot of help from Jehangir as well, as he himself believed that follow-up meant desperation. We had to work a lot on Jehangir's beliefs and coach him to look at follow-up as a customer's right and a salesman's duty. Through several examples and case studies we made him realize that a customer must feel valuable.

We believe it is the utmost duty of a salesman to make his or her customers feel liked, loved and respected. A simple phone call from a salesman can go a long way in building trust, respect and mutual understanding which is the foundation for any sale to happen. Imagine a salesman calling you, "Hello Mr. Kapoor, how are you? (waits for or the reaction) How are your wife and kids, sir? (waits for the reaction) Great! Hope you liked visiting our site yesterday... (waits for the reaction). It would be an honour to show your wife and kids around and learn their thoughts about an ideal home. What do you think, sir? (waits for the reaction) Would you like to bring them on Saturday afternoon at 4 pm or on Sunday morning at 11 am, sir? (waits for the reaction) I would love to have a coffee with you while they look around the entire township and see if it fits into their definition of an ideal home." Wouldn't you like that respect from any organization that you deal with? Of course yes! We like being liked and remembered and we guess so do you!

"But we are UCL" said Jehangir! The 'big brand mentality' was a big block and it ran through the veins and arteries of everyone at UCL. Being proud of your brand is one thing; making it an excuse for not taking action is completely different! Again it took a lot of coaching with Jehangir and the entire team to make them realize that it doesn't matter who you are! In fact, you should be taking the initiative of reaching out to your customers because of who you are – a big brand!

Our warning to Jehangir and team was this – Always remember that customers made us a big brand, only they have the power to. We can never become 'bigger' than our customers. We must reach out to them, make them feel they are liked, meet them at places where they feel it is convenient to and at times that are suitable to them. Otherwise, we will find ourselves in exactly the same spot where the nationalized banks had found themselves a few years ago – gigantic infrastructures, huge number of staff, multiple products, but *no new customers! As customers, we didn't find them friendly enough, so we said 'to hell with your brand' and moved on to open our accounts with private banks. The private banks flourished and kept adding customer-friendly services. Remember the days when we used to stand in queues to open a bank account! No more, the good guys come to our home now and help us open up an account right at the convenience of our home. On facing jolts on several fronts and on seeing private banks opening up branches by the thousands, some right next to them, the nationalized banks woke up to the need for customer-centricity. That was about ten years ago. Today several friends who have accounts with nationalized banks share stories of excellent customer service that they received and compare that with the ones they used to receive in the past. The nationalized banks are back in business again (barring a few laggards!).*

Once we had convinced Jehangir, it was easy convincing others including Sarfaraz. A change in mindset helped us challenge the unholy practice of labelling prospects as A, B or C. We had realized that it was far too counter-productive to the sales efforts. Thus began an era at UCL of treating prospects, no matter how small, as worthy of attention and respect.

To build on this mindset, we conducted several role plays in our training workshops to develop impactful follow-up skills. This helped the team to learn the fine difference between 'relationship-focused courteous follow-up' and 'sales-focused cranky pestering'.

One unproductive mindset overcome, we needed to move on to the next. We had to make Sarfaraz realize not to give too much importance to Jehangir's words, rather to focus on the intentions behind them. Jehangir wanted Sarfaraz to succeed, but given the pressures he was always working under, criticism came out naturally. Successful people are criticized too. However, they don't get stuck with the words, which generally are pretty harsh. Rather, they move on to find the intentions behind the criticism, the message underneath the words. As Sarfaraz learned the trick of dissociating Jehangir's intentions from his words, he began seeing the message clearly. He started asking Jehangir questions on objection-handling, working under pressure, closing deals constantly, identifying a prospect's needs, identifying all the people involved in the decision making process and so on and so forth. Jehangir was more than ready to help with the answers. These conversations helped Sarfaraz enhance his sales effectiveness which showed in his sales meetings. As the ability to build relationships increased, Sarfaraz's confidence increased. Increased confidence meant increase in sales and thus more confidence.

Today Sarafaraz doesn't communicate to impress people, he only communicates to express and to understand the other person's needs. He genuinely tries to see what he can offer to fulfil the other person's needs. 'This has not just improved my relations with customers, my team and my boss, but even relations with my friends and family. I have taken back my life's remote control from everyone I had given it to. So, only I decide how I want to feel at any given point of time. And since I love to feel motivated, that's how I feel most of the times now!'

Sarfaraz is now Senior Manager, Sales at UCL. He has two sales executives under him who are being groomed by Sarfaraz to become sales managers over a period of time, while Sarfaraz himself is being groomed by Jehangir to take up the position of DGM, Sales to assist him as his right hand.

FACING THIS TRUTH RIGHT NOW

Why do so many people believe in the lie 'my emotions and actions are controlled by people around me'? Why do they feel so sensitive to what people say? Why do get demotivated with every feedback they receive? Why do they get upset by what people say to them or how others behave with them? Well, there are several reasons why they do what they do. We are listing a few of them here. If you have felt sensitive to other people's opinion of you, which we are sure you have at some point of time (if not with everyone, there would at least be a few people whose words matter to you) you must read on to identify which reasons apply to you.

1. **A Complete Lack of Sense of Humor** – People who get upset with other people's words suffer from 'sensitivitis'. If you have sensitivitis, even in its mildest form, then you need a good dose of sense of humor. Sense of humor is not characterized by how quickly we can make fun of others and laugh at them. On the other hand, it is the ability to laugh at oneself and one's beliefs, the ability to find humor in situations, no matter how adverse they become and the ability to laugh at paradoxes present in the most revered institutions.

Anyone can crack a joke at others, only the great ones can laugh at themselves and their beliefs. When we crack jokes at others or point to the anomalies in other people's beliefs, that's called *satire*. But true humor is when we look at our own follies and are able to laugh them out.

Allow us to illustrate. Have you ever seen Amitabh Bachchan picking up a stone during a riot and throwing it at people of other religions? Have you ever seen Sachin Tendulkar burning a book because the author wrote something against his community? Have you ever heard Azeem Premji shouting slogans in front of a newspaper office because they printed an adverse article on the political leader he liked? Have you ever seen Ratan Tata burning tyres to protest against a film that depicted his Gods in a bad light? We can see that you're already smiling!

It is absolutely fine to be proud of one's culture, religion, family values, the school one attended, the gurus one believes in and so on and so forth. But you have to guard yourselves from allowing that pride to turn into arrogance, from allowing respect to turn into a *touchy-feely* topic. If you can laugh at the paradoxes within your own religion whether you are a Hindu, Muslim, Sikh, Jain, Christian or a Buddhist, you have expanded the limits of your sensitivity. If you can laugh at the weird anomalies that are present in your own society, in your neighborhood, in your family, in your friend circle and within you... you are close to freedom from sensitivitis!

We know of some amazing people who have found a vaccine for sensitivitis and have stayed miles away from this disease. The Dedhia brothers, Jagdish, Sanjay and Manish are directors of Mitsu Chem Pvt. Ltd., a rapidly growing organization in the plastic moulding industry. We haven't come across better examples of people who use humor to remain stress-free. The three brothers have a very sharp sense of humor and hence are able to laugh at themselves and the challenging situations they might find themselves in. '*Zindagi hasne-hasaane ke liye hai sir.*' (The purpose of life is to laugh and make others laugh) say the brothers.

Yes, laughter is STILL the best medicine!

2. **Lack of Focus on the Larger Goals** – Dr. APJ Abdul Kalam, one of the most popular presidents of India, has always been known for his inspiring speeches and visionary thoughts. Having completed his term as the President, Dr. Kalam was invited the world over as people from all walks of life wanted to hear him. Never a man to rest, Dr. Kalam travelled for 20-25 days across the globe. As an ex-President, Dr. Kalam is part of the list of people who are exempted

from security checks at all airports across the world. However, on the 29th of September 2009, he was frisked at the JFK Airport in America. There was a furore everywhere in India and the Indian authorities protested against the 'humiliation' inflicted by the American officials. The American government issued an apology to the Hon. Ex-President and 'deeply regretted the inconvenience'.

But, this was not the first time they had committed the mistake. He was frisked earlier by Continental Airlines officials in 2009 at New Delhi and had apologized then as well! How stupid and irresponsible you will say. And we agree. "They must be made to pay for their high-handed behaviour for disrespecting one of our role models," said a friend of ours. And we agreed.

But Dr. Kalam doesn't agree! On November 13th, 2011 he was confronted by journalists at Kolkata after he addressed the students of IIM there. He said, "Forget it. It is not worth talking about!"

Why doesn't he find it worth talking about? Because he has larger things to talk about – shaping India into a powerful nation, educating tomorrow's youth to become good citizens, bringing science and technology into the life of the common man and much more.

So much to learn from this man!

3. Mismatch between Ego and Self-image – In his book titled, *The High-Performance Entrepreneur* Subroto Bagchi while writing about how things changed during the 'IT Bubble Meltdown', shares how fake self-images can be self-destructing.

'In the last two years, I am amazed as to how many people we have bred who are not themselves. Every other day, I come across people who have a disproportionate image of themselves. Worse, they believe in the self-created image.

Some people look so puffed up. Strange job titles, phoney accents may look all right for a while. After some time, they can actually make a person unusable. The other day, I met an otherwise very usable middle level manager. Pre-meltdown he got carried away and got slotted for something he did not quite fit. His company is gone but he is still perched on that imaginary place. Even making conversation is so difficult with him because he helplessly mouths jargon that makes him look like a liability. It is important to be yourself. Fancy words on a resume do not carry one beyond a point. They actually destroy you.'

As mentioned earlier in the chapter *Break Free Truth 3 – In The Kick-Ass Format*, people become 'sensitive' when their ego is a bit bigger than their achievements can boast of. So in order to overcome *sensitivitis*, always let your achievements run ahead of your ego, not vice versa!

4. Inability to Segregate Intent from content – An example shared by Vijaya in one of her workshops on *Interpersonal Relationships and Networking Skills* for the managers of a leading multinational should explain the point we want to make.

As I was coaching a business owner, say, one Mr. Karan Gala in his forties who is a part of our Executive Coaching Program, he shared quite a few challenges related to his married life. "You must coach my wife, madam. She's always complaining. She says I don't love her anymore, that I have made life hell for her. She says I only think of my business and money. Her complaint is I don't spend enough time with her and the kids. How can she complain? She must know I'm doing all this if not for her and the kids, then for who else? My family means the world to me, but she doesn't understand. How am I going to give my best at work if I'm going to listen to all this every day? You must coach her to be more understanding of me." I paused and said, "Ok. This is what she said. What did you hear?" Mr. Gala looked puzzled, "Er... that's what she said... so that's what I heard... and I heard it right." I retaliated, "No, you didn't hear it right, sir. With all the criticism and allegations that she brought to the fore and with all the words she used, she didn't mean what she said."

"Then...?'" he asked. "Mr. Gala, your wife was saying, 'Sweetheart, I love you. You are the best friend and the only friend I have. I was afraid when I came to this family first. But, you understood me. I like spending time with you because you are the only one with whom I can be myself. I don't have to pretend to be anything other than me. So I yearn to be with you. Every morning when you leave, my heart feels blank; this entire home full of people makes me feel lonely. Every evening when the bell rings, I rush to the door expecting it to be you. And every time it turns out to be someone else, I feel frustrated. And when you come back in the evening, I feel like sharing everything that happened during the day. I feel like grabbing every moment with you and making the most out it. You are my best friend. I want my best friend back!' This is what she said. Now what did you hear, sir and who needs coaching?" Mr. Gala was taken aback. He couldn't utter a word for several minutes.

"But, it sounds so different, so positive when you say it, Vijaya ma'am. I can only hear all negative stuff when she speaks." he blurted. "Exactly my point sir! People around us are not communication experts. They are not trained at using the right words in the right order. So, it is our responsibility

> *to decode the message. It is our responsibility to focus on the 'intent' rather than the 'content'." Mr. Gala looked as if a lightning had struck him, "Yes, you are so right! People around me are not communication experts. They may say anything. But, I have to be more responsible in listening to the true message."*

Do we need to explain it further?

5. The desire to make everyone happy – This is probably the most common reason why people are very sensitive to what others say and feel. People trying to make everyone happy (like in the cases of W and Sarfaraz) end up making themselves unhappy in the long run.

In his 1977 classic *Anger – How to Live With And Without It*, Dr. Albert Ellis, the proponent of Rational Emotive Therapy wrote–

You cannot make everyone happy. Forget everyone; you cannot even make one person happy all the time! How true!

The desire to please everyone and make others happy results in submissive behaviour. On the other hand aggression might get you what you want, but will inevitably result in stressed relationships. Assertiveness is the only way out of the side-effects of submissiveness and aggressiveness. Assertiveness is the art of getting what you want without hurting others. Dr. Albert Ellis has suggested thirteen different methods to learn assertiveness. One of them is–

Risk saying no or refusing something yourself – Pick something that you usually don't want to do but that you often do in order to please others – such as going out to eat or carrying on a conversation for a long period of time – and deliberately take the risk of refusing to do this thing.

He goes on to mention that *'you can train yourself to act truly assertively, with responsibility towards yourself and others.'*

- Would you like to take back the remote control of your life?
- Would you like to feel in control in spite of all adversities like Avaram Baron?
- Would you like to feel in control of your emotions?
- Would you like to see your career soaring like Sarfaraz Hussain?
- Would you like to be able to focus on your larger goals like Dr. Kalam does?
- Would you like to hear what people really want to say rather than what appears to have been said?

LIVING THE TRUTH RIGHT NOW

The five reasons mentioned in the chapter *Facing This Truth Right Now* are also the 5 Tools that are needed in order to take back our life's remote control. So, the tools we require to be in control of our emotions are–

1. **Sharpen your sense of humor and use it to overcome sensitive feelings.**
2. **Focus on the larger goals when faced with discouraging words or behaviour.**
3. **Let your achievements run ahead of your ego.**
4. **Separate the Intent from the Content.**
5. **Make yourself happy first, using assertive behaviour.**

On the next page, write the names of at least five people whose words upset you or five situations that make you feel sensitive. These could be anyone, right from your husband / wife to your boss, or your customers or suppliers. In the next column, write what it is that they say or do that hurts you. In the next column write the tool you will select to counter the effect of those words or that behaviour (you can choose more than one). In the last column, write down the specific action you will undertake to take back the remote control of your life.

An example is given here to help you do the exercise on your own–

My Decision Sheet to take back my Life Remote Control

(Example)

Sr. No.	People/ Situations	What do they say / do that hurts / depresses me?	The Tools I'll Use to Counter Them	My Specific Action To Take Back My Life Remote Control
1.	Kavita, my wife	Compares my salary with that of the husbands of her friends	2. Focus on larger goals & 4. Separate Intent from Content	Next time I'll tell her, 'I appreciate your concern as I understand that you want me to be adequately compensated for all my hard work and competence. Let me assure you that I am in the right organization as this work makes me happy. I have defined a clear career growth plan and I'm following it. In the long run, I would have made far more money and name for myself than anyone you compare me with. So, let's go for a movie on that note?'

YOUR TRUTH 3   115

2	Oscar, my boss	Gives several things at a time, then points out the delay in my work in front of everyone else & demotivates me completely	3. Let your achievements run ahead of your ego. & 5. Make yourself happy first, using assertive behaviour.	Next time I'll say, 'I agree I'm running late and I'm extremely desirous of improving the delivery of tasks given to me. Will you be kind enough to share with me every morning which tasks you need finished on priority basis? We could discuss this in your cabin as I would like to note down all the feedback you have to offer.'
3	Siddharth, my son	Says my cooking is pretty ordinary thus hurting me	1. Sharpen your sense of humor and use it to overcome sensitive feelings. & 5. Make yourself happy first, using assertive behaviour.	Next time, I'll say, 'You are so right my boy. You see your mom was born to rule the world, not to cook dishes for you! Wrong job, what to do! But, you make me the Prime Minister of this country, and I'll run it so well. Until that time, this is what you'll get to eat' or I'll say, 'Ok, if you promise to increase your overall percentage by 10%, I'll improve my cooking by 20%! Deal?'

My Decision Sheet To Take Back My Life Remote Control

Sr. No.	People/ Situations	What do they say/ do that hurts/ depresses me?	The Tools I'll Use to Counter Them	My Specific Action To Take Back My Life Remote Control

4

Your Truth

4

One Should Always Speak One's Mind.

People are too sensitive...
I am very forthright by nature...
I don't keep anything in my heart...
I always say exactly what's on my mind ...
I don't mince words....
I can't be political or tactful...
I think being diplomatic is a waste of my time...
I am very transparent. What you see is what you get...
Don't expect me to beat around the bush...
I have no time to be nice. I would rather focus on getting things done...
Why do people feel bad when I call them an idiot when they actually are?

If the above is you, welcome to the 'I-speak-my-mind' Club. There are thousands of members in this Club too. They are the ones who are very proud of the fact that they are forthright and transparent. They don't believe in tactfulness and diplomacy. They're sure that saying nice words to others is highly political in nature. The gap between what they think and what they say is less than a micro second. And they take immense pride that they have a so-called clean heart. They wonder why they don't have great relationships with people, why their boss hates them, why their colleagues are so uncooperative, why they don't get enough opportunities and why people feel bad when they speak their mind. ('I have always been taught to speak the brutal truth.')

If you are one the members, which I suspect you are, welcome to the next Truth that will change your life.

What's Your Story?
Below this paragraph, you will find a table that is designed to enable you to face Your Truth.

Step 1
The Belief – Pick out one or similar sentences from the previous page that you have been uttering or thinking regularly.

Step 2
The Evidence – Write down at least one instance of why those sentences have been repeated by you so often.

Step 3
The Outcome – Write your feelings when you have proved that the sentences are your life's Truth.

The Belief ……..	The Evidence ……..

The Outcome ………

Step 4
Read on………….

THE STORY OF THE POWER OF WORDS

Mrs. D'souza was the most senior teacher at St. Anne's High School in Bangalore. She had spent the past 33 years teaching English at St. Anne's to higher secondary students. After having dedicated almost her entire life to teaching, which she didn't really enjoy quite as much, she was eagerly looking forward to her retirement which was due next year.

One day, the Principal of the school called a teachers' meeting and announced that the school was going to change its Board Affiliation from the next Academic Year. And in order to smoothly manage the transition of the syllabus, all the teachers were expected to undergo a two-week Teachers' Training Course. The teachers had been hearing about it for a few months but had not expected it to materialize so soon. Most of them were quite thrilled because the new system would create several opportunities for them to enhance their career.

Mrs. D'souza was the only one who marched into the Principal's office to protest against the training program. "After so many years of teaching, you think some girl barely out of her diapers is going to train me how to teach?" she stormed. "And anyway I just have 8 more months of teaching left before I retire. Why should I attend any training program? I refuse to attend it'" she declared. The Principal patiently heard all her objections and closed the meeting with the following words, "Mrs. D'souza, we all know that you know your subject well, but if you do not get a certificate of completion for this Training Program, I am afraid we will be unable to continue utilizing you as a teacher for the next academic year. As per the rule of the new board, all teachers need to qualify under the new system before they can be given their re-appointment letters."

A very disgruntled D'souza Teacher enrolled herself for the course after having promised herself that she would not listen to a single word that the trainer said. Feeling better after her promise, she then proceeded to do exactly what her students had done for so many years. She occupied the last bench, doodled her name on the writing pad, she gazed out of the window, she daydreamed, she kicked the teacher sitting in front of her, she passed chits to her classmates and dozed in the afternoons, while the trainers continued to orient the class in new evolved methods of teaching, use of technology in the classroom, the psychology of today's generation and the multiple roles of today's teachers.

It was the second last day and Mrs. D'souza was waiting for the course to get over so that she could get back to life, secretly admitting to herself that it hadn't been too bad. Just before the facilitator was about to disperse for the day, she declared, "There is homework for all of you today." She smiled when she heard the groans. "Take a piece of paper and write down your name on it," she instructed, "Then write down the name of the worst student that you have had to deal with in your life as a teacher."

While all the teachers racked their brains to identify their worst students, Mrs. D'souza didn't have to think too much. She scribbled the name that still made her anxious – Sonia Sharma.

We all remember our worst experiences with people more than our good ones. And Mrs. D'souza wasn't wrong when she wrote Sonia's name. Sonia was a child from a broken home. She was a sulky child, whose childhood was one of abuse and violence. Her father was an alcoholic and often absent for long periods of time. Her mother was an indifferent one and Sonia's earliest memories were of physical beatings and fights at home between her parents, whenever her father was home. Her mother, a ravishing beauty in her youth, found solace in the arms of other men, each one more notorious than the other. Sonia constantly saw a string of strange men in and out of her house and her mother's guilt-ridden despair and tears after every romantic episode. Children from such homes, as you all know, deal with the situation usually in two extreme ways. Either they become submissive and fearful or they turn aggressive and violent. Sonia was the latter.

Being deprived of attention at home, she was an attention grabber at school. She would bully younger children, beat them up, snatch their lunch boxes and tear up their books. In class, she would disturb the other children and disrupt the classroom with her irrelevant questions and obnoxious behaviour with the teachers. She was a terror and teachers would silently pray for her absence from their class – which seldom happened, because Sonia never missed her classes or an opportunity to create hell for others. A naturally intelligent child, she made sure that her marks enabled her to move up to the next class without making any effort to outperform or outshine her classmates.

As Sonia entered her adolescence, she suddenly discovered other ways of grabbing attention. Her speech was deliberately peppered generously with slang and abuse. She would do all kinds of things to attract boys' attention. She would ask questions in class that made teachers blush to the roots of their hair. Her conversations were filled with innuendos and she was the despair of every teacher who had the misfortune of teaching her class.

At the age of 13, when she was in the eighth grade, the peon of the school caught her smoking in the grounds behind the school. He grabbed her and dragged her to the Principal's *office. The Principal immediately called up Sonia's mother and requested her to take her child back home as the school was intolerant of such disruptive behaviour. This wasn't the first time the mother had been called to the Principal's office and it wasn't the first time either that she sobbed and begged the Principal to give her daughter one more chance at reforming. The Principal, a kind-hearted woman, who knew the circumstances of Sonia's home, admonished her and instructed her to keep Sonia away from mischief.*

Sonia was back at school the next day, with the same attitude and a whole new set of bruises to show for the incident. A few months passed. And then one day, when she was 14, in the ninth grade, she was caught by a teacher in the faculty room, trying to change the marks on her report card. Now this was too much. A livid teacher and a sulking Sonia had an audience again with the Principal. This time the mother shed even more tears and begged the teacher and the Principal to give her daughter just one more chance. "What will she do at home?" she cried. "Even for the most ordinary of jobs, she would need to have finished at least her schooling. Please don't rusticate her, ma'am. You know our situation. Her entire life is in your hands. I swear she will not give you another chance to complain. I beg you. I cannot manage her. I give you complete permission to deal with her in the manner you deem fit. But please don't remove her from school. She just has one more year to go," she sobbed.

A resigned Principal, shooed them out of her room, deeply pondering on the future of such a child, thankful that there was just one Sonia Sharma in her school.

The next year, Sonia was in Mrs. D'souza's class. Mrs. D'souza, well aware of Sonia's reputation from the other teachers, prepared herself mentally to deal with her. And she was not disappointed. Sonia's behaviour was as shocking as expected in the class. Mrs. D'souza disliked her on sight and made up her mind to ignore her for the rest of the year. She was a good teacher and the class was full of good students (other than Sonia, of course) and the months flew past.

One day, Sonia fainted in class. A worried Mrs. D'souza took her to the school health centre and was taken aback when she heard the doctor's verdict. Sonia, all of 15 years of age, was pregnant. The next few hours was a flurry of activities, what with the call to Sonia's mother, the meeting with the Principal, the explanations to the other teachers, the ranting and raving of Mrs. Sharma at Sonia and then the silently fuming mother dragging her daughter out of the school. That had been the last that Mrs. D'souza had heard of Sonia and she had shelved the memory, as life had continued a little more easily for her.

This was the Sonia Sharma whose name Mrs. D'souza had scribbled on the paper that the trainer had requested. The trainer proceeded to collect all the chits from the teachers ensuring that they had filled in their own name, and told them what the homework was. "Contact the person whose name you have written. Speak to them. Ask them about how they have been. And if you can think of any good quality that the child might have had, tell him / her about it. We will discuss your experience tomorrow morning in the class."

Mrs. D'souza protested, "Excuse me, dear. That student was in my class almost 17 years back. How am I supposed to contact her? I would like to change the name. Should I submit another chit?"

The trainer smiled, "No. The name cannot be changed. See you tomorrow morning. Have a good evening," and she walked out of the classroom.

Mrs. D'souza's mind was working furiously to find an easy way out of this. "Aha! The school records," she thought, "I will definitely find Sonia's home address and phone number there." But surprise! The school only had records of students who had passed out 15 years back. A grumbling Mrs. D'souza, on her way home, hit upon another idea. Rajeev Sankpal, who had been in the same batch as Sonia, had been regularly sending her Christmas cards from America. She decided to contact him for Sonia's number.

On reaching home, without wasting a moment, she rummaged through her old mails and after digging into shoe boxes filled with letters and plastic bags filled with cards, she found Rajeev's number. She looked at the clock and mentally calculated the 13 hour gap between the Indian Standard Time and its counterpart in USA, which made it around 06.30 am. "Time to wake up," she thought as she dialled Rajeev's number. It was a delighted and very surprised Rajeev who answered the phone when Mrs. D'souza introduced herself. And he was even more surprised when she told him the reason for her call. "That type of girl could never be my friend, ma'am," he said, "but I have the number for Neeta who used to be Sonia's friend. I am sure you remember her. Perhaps she may have her number. She is in Bombay. Wait, let me get it for you." He gave her Neeta's number and promised to visit her when he was next in Bangalore, before hanging up.

Mrs. D'souza stared at the number in her hand. She then proceeded to call Neeta. Neeta picked up the phone, "Hello". "Hello. Is this Neeta from St. Anne's high school? I am Mrs. D'souza. I used to be your class teacher. Do you remember me?" Mrs. D'souza asked. "Eeeee! Hi ma'am. What a lovely, lovely surprise! I used to love the way you used to teach us. How come you have my number? How can I help you?" Neeta gushed into the phone. A pleased Mrs. D'souza replied, "I believe you used to be Sonia Sharma's friend. Can you give me her number?" There was complete silence on the other end of the line, except for the sound of a TV playing music in the distance and the faint sounds of children laughing in the background. "I don't have her number," Neeta snapped, "Why would you think I had it?" "I... I... am sorry. I thought you two had been best friends," stuttered Mrs. D'souza. "She was. And I wish that I had never met her," said Neeta, her voice strangely strained, as though she had a lump in her throat, "I thought of her as a sister. She spent her entire day with me and my family. I shared everything I had with her – my food, my clothes, my shoes – not knowing that she would think of that as permission to share the bed with the man I truly loved, Sanjay. She hurt me terribly and I have recovered from that pain after a long time. I am now married to a wonderful man and have two lovely kids. But I will never forgive her."

Now it was Mrs. D'souza's turn to be quiet. "I don't have her number," Neeta continues, "But I have Sanjay's number. You can contact him but please don't tell him that you got the number from me," she said as she rattled off a mobile number from memory. Mrs. D'souza slowly hung up the phone and dialled Sanjay's number.

The phone was picked up by a man having a lovely deep voice, "Hello." "Hello. My name is Mrs. D'souza. And I am a teacher at St. Anne's in Bangalore. Am I speaking to Sanjay?" she asked. "Yes, ma'am. How can I help you?" he asked pleasantly. Mrs. D'souza tentatively asked, "I believe you know a girl called Sonia Sharma. Can you please give me her phone number? She used to be in my class and I need to contact her." She could almost feel the ice creeping into his voice, as he barked, "Who gave you my number? I knew her, but *sometimes I feel that I never truly did. She was the bitch who made me cheat on the most wonderful girl in the world, took away my money, created a rift between me and my family and made me lose three years of my studies because I truly loved her. And what did I get in return? She just slept with my best friend and left me for good." "I am so sorry, son," Mrs. D'souza said softly, "This call must have hurt you terribly. I didn't mean to. I just wanted her phone number." "I don't have her number. But I have the name of the company where she used to work in Bangalore till a couple of years back. The company's name is GG Exports. Now please don't call me back. Ever," he said, before banging the phone down.*

A very subdued Mrs. D'souza looked up the number of GG Exports in the telephone directory and dialled it. "Hello. Good evening. Thich ich GG Egchpot Kompnee," said a voice. "Hello. My name is Mrs. D'souza. I am a teacher at St. Anne's School. I am trying to trace a student of mine, named Sonia Sharma, who I believe is working in your company. Can you please help me with her phone number?" Mrs. D'souza asked. "Shorry, Madam," the man replied in broken English, "I'm de Sekuritee Gard. The ladee dat you naming vark 'ere two year befor. I vas dooty 'ere and katch 'er shtealing from vare'ouse. I kall de police. De police take 'er avay." "Oh dear!," Mrs. D'souza exclaimed, "Can I contact her in any way?" "I giv u 'er mudder number from log buk. She kum to tak police shtashun address," he said. And he proceeded to look for the log book and gave her Sonia's mother's number after keeping Mrs. D'souza hanging on to the phone for over 10 minutes.

By now, Mrs. D'souza was exhausted. But she willed herself to call Mrs. Sharma, sure that at least Sonia's mother would have some kind words to say about her daughter. She was in for a shock.

After introducing herself and feeling pleased at Mrs. Sharma's recognition and warm response, she proceeded to ask her for Sonia's phone number. What she heard chilled her heart because never had she expected a mother to spit so much venom against her own child. "I consider my daughter dead. I hope she dies a horrible death. I hope she suffers the way I am suffering. You know how much trouble I have had in my life and the amount of sacrifices that I have made for her. About two years ago, I even sold my jewellery to bail her from jail. And what do I get from that ungrateful wretch when I call her to help me out? I have been suffering from cancer for the past two years and I begged her to take care of me. But she has disappeared. Hasn't called me up even once since the day I told her about my illness. I wouldn't wish a daughter like her on even my enemy. I have disowned her and I don't really care whether she is dead or alive," she said bitterly, her voice filled with an unknown emotion. "This is her number. But don't expect her to be there," she said as she spewed out a landline number before hanging up.

The time was 11.30 in the night. A tired and dispirited Mrs. D'souza called up the number in her hand. The phone rang a dozen times before disconnecting. "That's it!" Mrs. D'souza exclaimed in frustration, "I refuse to make any more calls. Ridiculous exercise. I will tell the trainer what I think of her stupid homework and her so-called training. A complete waste of my time and energy. And what a depressing evening." She then made herself some dinner, had a bath, changed into her nightclothes and went to bed.

She tossed and turned for the next couple of hours. "What will I tell the trainer? She will make me look like a fool in front of all the other teachers for not completing my homework. And though true, my excuse does sound pathetic. What do I say – that my student did not pick up her phone?" she fretted because all her life she had heard hundreds of excuses for non-completion of homework. "Teacher, I did my homework, but my sister vomited on it." "Teacher, I did my homework, but the dog ate it up." "Teacher, I swear I did my homework, but I forgot my book at home." "Teacher, my homework was right on this page, but now it has disappeared."

So, "Teacher, I called up Sonia, but she didn't pick up the phone," didn't sound good enough. Finally, unable to sleep, she thought of trying Sonia's number one last time. The time was about 2.30 am.

The phone kept ringing, and as a relieved Mrs. D'souza was just about to hang up, a woman answered the phone with an abrupt hello.

Mrs. D'souza was taken aback. She really hadn't expected the phone to be picked up.

"Hello," she said, "Is this Sonia?"

"Yeah," Sonia replied rudely, "Have you seen the time?"

"I am so sorry to be disturbing you at this time, dear. I am Mrs. D'souza. I used to be your class teacher", Mrs. D'souza said.

"So?" Sonia replied.

A completely flustered Mrs. D'souza, who at least expected a Hello-how-are-you-how-nice-of-you-to-call, stuttered, "I was thinking the entire evening about you. And I thought I should call you up to ask you how you are." Hearing complete silence at the other end, and for lack of anything else to say, she continued, "I was thinking about how tough your life had been when you were a child. And how you coped with it." Hearing no reply from Sonia, she giggled nervously, "I...

I... still remember how we were all terrified of you. And your sheer guts and devil-may-care-attitude always amazed me. I... I... um... thought that you were damn brave to be coming to school and facing the world in spite of your... ah... unconventional life" she ended lamely. But Sonia had hung up the phone before Mrs. D'souza had even completed her sentence.

A livid Mrs. D'souza, banged the phone back on its cradle and cursed everyone she could think of – the school, the Principal, the trainer, the training, the Board of Trustees and of course, the shameless and wretched breed of today's children who hadn't even the courtesy to show gratitude. Manner-less pigs, she concluded, before wrapping herself in her blanket and going off to sleep.

The next day, fully equipped with her battle gear, she reached school early, wanting to accost the trainer before the others arrived. She had rehearsed all the rude things she would say. And she was tapping her foot impatiently for the trainer to enter the classroom, when the security guard knocked on the door and walked in. "Good morning, teacher," he said reverently, before putting an envelope on her table, "This letter was left for you today early in the morning by a lady." And he walked out closing the door behind him.

Mrs. D'souza stared at the envelope and then picked it up with trembling hands. Her name was scrawled on the envelope which contained a single sheet of paper. She read the letter addressed to her:

"Dear D'souza ma'am,

    I don't know what miracle prompted you to call me up yesterday night. It was my birthday. And I have never *felt lonelier. I hadn't received a single call the entire day. No one knew or even cared whether I was dead or alive. I had no one in the world who loved me, cared for me or even thought of me. I guess you will never understand the depths of despair that I have been feeling now for many months. I have driven away everyone who loved me and I have made mistakes in my life that I am ashamed to even think about. I was tired of living. When you called, I had a bottle of vodka in one hand and a bottle of sleeping pills in the other. I was going to end my life.*

And then your miraculous call came. Reminding me that there are people who still think of me. That I have faced tougher circumstances in the past. After the call, I sat and thought for a very long time. And I have decided to recreate my life using the same things that I had forgotten that I had – guts, courage and attitude. I am going to see my mother today as I am missing her terribly. I am going to ask her for her forgiveness for being a horrible daughter and take care of her for the rest of her life. She is very ill. There are too many people I have hurt. And I am going to make amends. I will be in touch. I will come to see you once I have achieved something to be proud of.

Thank you for your call. Thank you for your words.

Love,

Sonia Sharma

Mrs. D'souza was wiping her tears as she folded the letter back into the envelope, just as you are wiping yours.

THE POWER OF WORDS – DECODED

- What was Mrs. D'souza's reaction when she was forcibly sent for the Training Program?
- What was her reaction when she didn't hear courteous words from Sonia?
- What was Sonia's reaction to what Mrs. D'souza said?
- And what was her reaction when she read Sonia's letter?

We guess you're getting the point. Kind words come back as a reward for speaking kindly to others. People start understanding us once we take the pain to understand who they are and why they are the way they are.

A few kind words from Mrs. D'souza saved one life! That's the power of words – our words can make or break someone's life. Mrs. D'souza could have said all the nasty things about Sonia that she had just heard over the telephone. Yet she chose to speak of one good quality that she had observed in Sonia – courage. Communication skills are not about all the words we know in any language, not about the vocabulary, nor the diction or the grammar! It is about how we use those words and when.

BREAK FREE TRUTH 4

One should always speak keeping the other in mind.

BREAK FREE TRUTH 4 – IN A 'KICK-ASS' FORMAT

Ok. Wipe your eyes and your snivelling nose. And let's get to the point. You have hurt too many people with what you have said in the past. Right? And if you are one of those who is still justifying why your 'forthright' stance is correct, here is the truth in a "kick-ass" format. You want straight talk? You got it, mate.

Imagine you going for a walk. And there is this street dog who has decided that it does not like you. Can't help it. You haven't had a good day and it is showing on your face. What do you think it would do?

Of course, it will bark at you.

Then not satisfied with just the bark (you gave it a dirty look and it wasn't appreciated), it decides to chase you right out of its neighbourhood. What did you think it would do?

Of course, it will chase after you.

And it caught up with you (You never stood a chance anyway). And while you promised yourself and God that if ever you got out of this unscathed, you will join the gym and participate in the Standard Chartered Marathon, the dog decides to help itself to one big juicy chunk of that unwanted bulk that you have been sporting. Now what did you think it would do?

Of course. it will do right that – BITE YOU.

Because the dog believes in keeping a clean heart and not keeping anything bottled up inside and is very forthright and frank. It does what it thinks. No time wasted on sensitivity, kindness, beating around the bush, modifying the words to appeal to you… and things like that.

So, you see, being frank and brutally true with people kind of puts you in the wild animal category. Because if you think about it, humans are the only breed that have the capacity to think, the boon of words and the skill to weave their words into sentences that can connect. Animals don't. So be human(e).

THE 5 BREAK FREE TRUTHS TRACKER - WEEK 4

Your Truth - one should always speak one's mind.
My Truth - one should always speak keeping the other in mind.

What I Believed – My Truth	*I always was very proud of the fact that I am a very forthright person. And that I never keep anything in my mind. That people are too sensitive. "Call a spade, a spade. And an idiot, an idiot," was my philosophy of life. I was always proud of my linguistic skills, not realizing that my communication skills are extremely poor.*
What The Truth Is – My Realizations	*Sonia Sharma's story brought tears to my eyes, when I realized that I must have hurt so many people by saying the wrong things to them. By not having the sensitivity to say kind, generous, inspiring things to them. I have now realized that words matter.*
My Next Step	*I will read up or attend a program on communication skills. Not because my language needs correction, but because my usage of the language does. I will consciously script what I am going to say to people, so that I can express my thought in a manner that is simple, clear, respectful and sensitive to their feelings.*
My Truth Partner	*Anuradha Gupta (Wife)*

THE 5 BREAK FREE TRUTHS TRACKER – WEEK 4

Your Truth – one should always speak one's mind.
My Truth – one should always speak keeping the other in mind.

What I Believed – My Truth	
What The Truth Is – My Realizations	
My Next Step	
My Truth Partner	

OUR EXPERIENCES WITH THE 'TRUTH'

This is an incident from the lives of our clients Mr. Rasik Shah, Mr. Chintan Shah and Mr. Amit Gulati (names changed). The three are close friends from college and are the Directors of Rajashri Engineering Pvt. Ltd. which they started immediately after graduating from the university. Their friendship is 27 years old and their company is 23 years old. Rajashri Engineering is into the business of construction, especially high-rise towers and commercial spaces. Larger construction houses and builders outsourced their construction jobs to them. Their high degree of commitment saw their organization move from being an all-friends outfit to a large corporation with more than two hundred people working.

As business grew, the friends found themselves increasingly inept at managing the complexities of the large corporation. They were engineers who were good at building towers, but they had never built any teams. In spite of having 200 people working for them, they were the busiest of all. They would arrive at work before everyone and would mostly be found locking the office several hours after everyone had left. Their construction sites needed their presence for things to run smoothly. To make matters worse, several clients would delay payments for months at a stretch leaving the organization cash-strapped. They were fighting the battle on several fronts and yet reaching nowhere. They had too much on their shoulders and it was bound to show somewhere. And so it did!

The first thing to get affected was the relationships. Mr. Chintan Shah felt Mr. Amit Gulati was too lenient with clients in not asking for timely payments. Mr. Gulati felt Mr. Chintan Shah was ineffective in completing projects on time; hence the clients were not paying on time. Mr. Rasik Shah felt that the need of the hour was recruiting competent project managers and delegating the task of project management. Matters went from bad to worse when Mr. Chintan Shah refused to attend the directors' meetings on the grounds that his opinion was not considered before making payments to vendors. It was an explosive situation. The three directors had stretched matters to the extent of threatening to go solo if the others didn't budge.

In our executive coaching sessions individually with the directors, all we could hear from them was how things were not working and how unreasonable the other two directors were. There was too much at stake... 200 families, on-going projects, organization's reputation etc., etc, Of course, we couldn't be mere spectators.

At this point, we called a joint meeting of the three directors and allowed them to speak their mind. Each one shared their version of the story and felt that other two did not understand enough. Allegations were made and tempers rose, walk-outs happened and accusations were exchanged. But we didn't allow the meeting to end there.

While each one wanted the others to understand him, our agenda was to make them realize that all the three had to understand the others first. While each one wanted to speak their mind our struggle was to make them realize that all the three had to speak keeping the others in mind first. It was a marathon meeting that lasted for more than seven hours and our patience paid off.

As the three friends vented out their feelings for nearly two hours, they began cooling down and listening to the others more attentively. Our mediation helped as they were forced to write down any valid feedback given by the other directors and promise to look at it differently, if not accept it completely. Two shorter reconciliatory meetings after the marathon meeting and matters came back to pretty normal. Mr. Chintan Shah accepted the responsibility for the delay in project execution and presented an action plan to finish projects within the deadlines set by various clients. He even agreed to recruit two new project managers and delegate a few responsibilities to them.

Mr. Amit Gulati presented an action plan to improve collections. In fact, before the third meeting he had met several key clients and sent reminder letters to a few others. It seemed to work as money had started to come in. Mr. Rasik Shah took over the responsibility of managing one project from Mr. Chintan Shah and also proposed to follow-up for payments with a few clients.

It's been four years since that day and Rajashri Engineering has expanded. They've not just taken up more projects in India, but overseas as well. In fact, this year they have launched residential projects under their own brand name. Rajshri Engineering is not just a construction company now, it's a Group of Companies with varied business interests.

Having strategically developed several systems and processes to streamline operations and accounts, the directors seem more relieved and are able to spend more quality time with each other... as friends!!!

FACING THIS TRUTH RIGHT NOW

Dr. David Schwartz in his bestseller *The Magic of Thinking Big* has an important piece of advice for all those who want to achieve success in life –*Don't waste time or mental energy trying to classify people as 'very important persons', 'important persons' or 'unimportant persons'. Make no exceptions. A person, whether he is a garbage collector or a company vice-president, is important to you. Treating someone as second-class never gets you first-class results.*

We agree. Relationships – whether they are with the most affluent and powerful in our society or with those that are at the lowest stratum in society are equally important. Both of us have worked hard in building, maintaining and preserving relationships with people of every class and creed and have reaped tremendous benefits out of the same.

However, we are by no means implying that all our relationships have been equally effective. Just like us, each one of you has certain relations that are strained or are not working as effectively as we would want them to. Maybe you have an estranged uncle, aunt, cousin, your ex-boss, or an old client where things just didn't go right or a vendor who lost your trust or a subordinate who forgot you in spite of your training and mentoring, or a teacher who has made a difference to your life and whom we simply haven't connected with, or your mother on whom you have always rudely hung up the phone because you're too busy to speak to her… or your father with whom you haven't spoken at all!

- Would you like to have the amazingly positive outcome like the three friends for all your strained relations?
- Would you like to see people treating you kindly and with respect?
- Would you like to create an impact in the lives of a few people right now?
- Would you like to make someone sleep peacefully tonight?
- Would you like to sleep peacefully tonight?

LIVING THE TRUTH RIGHT NOW

Write at least three names of people with whom who have estranged relations / relations that you intend to improve. Write what you are going to tell them. Remember, even Amitabh Bachchan needs a script.

What should you say? Nothing much – just tell the person you were thinking about him / her and share anything positive you might have noticed about him / her. Mind you,anything positive! There's no need to fix the blame on who caused strain in the relationship, no need to apologize and no need to ask for an apology either! No need to explain. No need to listen to explanations.

You will realize once you make the call, that all these activities are pretty redundant in mending broken relationships or in improving the existing ones.

Person 1 ....

Script ....

....

....

....

....

Person 2 ....

Script ....

....

....

....

....

Person 3 ....

   Script ....

....

....

....

....

Now pick up your phone and make that long-due call right away. You could be Mrs. D'souza in someone's life. You could bring about a smile on someone's face, or peace in someone's disturbed life or infuse the much-needed energy in a dispirited soul! Make the phone call right away.

But, beware! You may get pretty weird reactions –

Denial – Of course I am not hurt...

Acceptance – I always knew that...

Disbelief – Is everything ok? Not going to commit suicide after this call, are you?

Reciprocal – I also want to tell you how wonderful you are....

Silence.

You don't worry about their reactions. You just do your duty of telling them what you have scripted, though the temptation to veer from the script will be very high.

Once you have made the phone call, write down your experience on the next page in terms of what you are feeling. What are you waiting for? Keep the book down right now. Pick it up only when you have spoken to all the three people you have named. No cheating!

Best of luck!

My Experience

I spoke to _____

They're feeling – _____

I am feeling – _____

I spoke to _____

They're feeling – _____

I am feeling – _____

I spoke to _____

They're feeling – _____

I am feeling – _____

5

Your Truth

5

I Can't...

I can't work harder than that.
I can't achieve my promotion.
I can't lose weight. Impossible.
It is not possible for me to exceed this year's target.
I can't stay back late.
I can't travel.
I can't learn English now at my age.
I can't take up a full time job, even though I need the money.
I can't spend more time with my family.
I can't build a world-class organization.
I can't ask my accountant to resign, even though I know that he is
*   cheating me.*
I can't recruit a CEO.
I can't double my sales turnover this year.
I can't make my life simpler.
I can't find time to spend on myself.
I can't be a better husband / wife / father / son.
I can't save money.
I can't buy a house.
I can't go for a holiday.
I can't speak in public.
I can't take up that job offer because I can't live without my family.
I can't give up smoking.
I can't learn music at my age.
It's too late. I can't restart my career.
I can't give up drinking.

I can't help you because I am helpless.
I can't go for a trek.
I can't dance.
I can't be confident.
I can't buy a car.
I can't work on a computer.
I can't run the marathon.
I can't cook.
I can't take care of myself.
I can't manage all this by myself.
I can't... I can't... I can't...

If the above is the story of your life, welcome to the 'I-Can't' Club. This Club has the largest number of people in it. Almost every person you meet will be at least a part-time member of this club. These are the people who see obstacles in everything. Their first reaction to any opportunity is 'I can't'. Hundreds of opportunities come their way and they never realize it. And then they wonder why others are more successful than them.

They have been programmed since their childhood that anything that looks difficult, actually *is*. And anything that is even remotely unconventional is 'impossible'. They are so aghast at doing anything that is beyond their comfort zone that they become the greatest obstacles to their own success.

Are you one of them?

Whats Your Story?
Below this paragraph, you will find a table that is designed to enable you to face Your Truth.

Step 1
The Belief – Pick out one or similar sentences from the previous page that you have been uttering or thinking regularly.

Step 2

The Evidence – Write down at least one instance of why those sentences have been repeated by you so often.

Step 3

The Outcome – Write your feelings when you have 'proved' that the sentences are your life's Truth.

The Belief	The Evidence ....

The Outcome ....

Step 4

Read on.............

You are in for a bumper of stories in this section. There were too many examples and we simply did not know which ones to reject. So, you are going to get more than what you bargained for.

Six People

Three Stories

Two Philosophies

One Truth.

THE STORY OF TWO ARTISTS

It was the late 1960s. Popularity of movies was increasing by the day. Suddenly there were 'talkies' emerging everywhere. And there was rarely a person in the entire country that hadn't seen a film. Parents were naming their children after movie stars, while every young boy was adopting colorful scarves around his neck and every young girl was styling her hair into a bouffant. The cinema industry was at its peak and directors were experimenting with different actors and actresses to capitalize on this new and exciting journey of entertainment.

This was a time when everyone wanted to become a movie star. And this is a story about two young, talented, hardworking boys, who dreamed of stardom – Aniket and Ranjan.

Aniket and Ranjan were a complete contradiction to each other. While Aniket was from a small town in Bihar with parents who were poor farmers, Ranjan was the son of a successful industrialist from Mumbai (Bombay then). Aniket was dark, very tall and lanky, with ordinary features, while Ranjan was fair (you can imagine how that worked in his favor in the light of our national obsession with fairness), well-built and stylish. Aniket had no one to guide him, while Ranjan's father had employed the best of talent to give his son the exposure that would propel him to stardom. Aniket went hungry for several days at a time, having no source of income, while Ranjan's extravagant parties were the talk of the town.

It was sheer fate that they ended up working in the same movie. Aniket had been, as usual along with a dozen others, waiting outside the gates of the film studio, in the hope of catching the eye of one of the directors. The door opened and one of the production assistants came out. He had a sheet in his hand and as he scanned the crowd of young boys his eyes fell on Aniket. "Hey you," he shouted above the noise pointing at Aniket, "Come inside. We want a tall, thin man to play the role of a sick brother to the hero." Aniket played the role of the sick brother (supposed to be a two-minute affair originally) so well that the director extended his role in the movie. This was the same movie in which Ranjan was making his debut as the hero. And the rest was history.

They both won awards for their performance that year at the Annual Film Awards. Aniket became the hero of the masses, while Ranjan became the icon of the classes. They were paired together in several movies as protagonists fighting for opposite causes. While Aniket played the role of the broody, intense hero to perfection, Ranjan wooed the audience with his charm, his good looks and his romantic image. They were the darling of the media and the public. Heroines languished if they weren't cast against them and producers were willing to invest any amount to get them to sign up for movies under their banner. Aniket and Ranjan were living their dream and life was perfect.

And then the 1980s arrived.

By then both were in their early forties. Ranjan was still inundated with scripts that offered him challenging roles – middle-aged hero, family man, elder brother, father and the main villain. He refused every script where he wasn't playing the main lead as a romantic. His response was, "I can't play the role of older men. I am a romantic at heart. I have a reputation to consider. The audience has always loved me in the role of a dashing, charming rake. I can't take roles where I am playing serious characters. I can't do it."

Aniket, too had several scripts which required him to now play roles which he had never played before – a rich brother, a burdened family man, an antagonistic father and in several *cases a cold criminal. The change in the characterization was a painful one. Aniket spent sleepless nights rehearsing his new avatar. From being the central figure around which the movie revolved, he now was known for his character roles. Whenever an opportunity arose for him to play a character which he had never played before, he told himself a thousand times, "I can do it", like a litany.*

Ranjan, always having suffered from genetic obesity issues, now started filling out. There came a time, when he was unable to move without help. For every diet that the doctor prescribed, for every exercise the physiotherapist recommended, Ranjan had a standard answer, "I can't. Don't expect me to control my diet. And I have never exercised in my life before. I can't start it now."

Aniket, who had discovered a long time ago that he had a medical history of diabetes in his family, brought in a rigorous change in his lifestyle, his eating habits and his exercise regime. He worked hard, but not at the cost of his health. Not that he wasn't tempted to binge on sweets or laze around after an especially grueling day. But to every temptation he would tell himself, 'I can resist this.'

Then there came a time when even these roles fizzled out for both Aniket and Ranjan. Ranjan had a good source of income due to his family's other businesses and he started living a life of rest and relaxation. Aniket, now in his 50s, had no doubt that if he stopped working, the funds that he had managed to create so carefully over several years would fizzle out. So he started working for whatever assignments came his way – commercials, print ads, guest appearances... in spite the advice of many of his friends and relatives to 'take it easy'.

When the producers of a large production house, were on the lookout for a senior host for a live reality show on television, Ranjan's family members encouraged him to speak to the producer. They were sure that his talent, charm and wit would find a ready platform for expression. But he refused with his, now embedded, response, "I can't. Movies were different. How can I host a reality show on television? I have never done it before and I am sure I can't do it now. And I definitely can't call the producer and beg for the role. What will people say? I have my reputation to consider."

When Aniket heard about this, he fortified his heart against rejection and made a call to the producer. After several meetings, Aniket was offered the role for hosting the show, though some of the producers had their reservation about the same. "I CAN do it," Aniket assured them, "I will ensure that you get your money's worth. If not, then don't pay me a penny". And then went on to become the most famous anchor in the history of television.

The last I heard, Ranjan, now in his seventies, has had a stroke because of his obesity, is comatose because of all the medication that he now needs to consume to stay alive and is now living at the mercy of his relatives and other family members, having run through his inheritance a long time back.

And Aniket, who recently celebrated his seventy-fifth birthday, is authoring a book based on his experiences in the film industry, is shooting for an average of 3 movies every year, has about 50 commercials to his credit in the past several years, is once again a household name for his super-appreciated anchoring of television's longest running reality show and continues to be the favorite actor for three generations in a row. When people tried to draw a parallel about his success with other co-stars' failures, he was too busy to comment.

THE STORY OF TWO TALENTED WOMEN

Priti and Anita have been friends since school. Both were from middle class families and like all middle class parents, theirs too encouraged them to learn various arts and perform in school and college events. Both were talented and good students. And it wasn't a surprise, when they both represented their school and later their college in inter-school and college events and festivals.

Priti and Anita continued their student life with unstoppable successes, both in events and in admirers. They were, if not at the top of their class in academics, top of the list when it came to popularity. Teachers and other students, alike, were sure that Priti and Anita would make a mark in the corporate world. By the time they finished their graduation, they had a line of proposals for marriage and also a list of offers from good organizations for their career. Their extremely proud parents told them to choose their own life partner and the job of their choice. And they both did just that.

Anita joined a renowned company where she started working as a junior assistant. Being pretty, talented and hardworking, it wasn't surprising that her boss proposed marriage to her. He was from a good family; was ambitious, well-educated and good-looking to boot. Though they were not from the same caste, the parents, unwillingly at first, gave their blessings for the marriage. Anita then joined a small organization that was closer to her home, even though the salary was lower and the job itself was not very challenging. When her friends tried to reason with her and advised her not to change her job, she replied, "I can't manage to travel that far. I have to manage both home and work now." Anita soon settled down to a life of home, work and innumerable social events.

In a couple of years, she was given the opportunity of going abroad for a project. The project was for two months and when her superior recommended her name, she shook her head. "I can't travel. I have too many commitments at home." "At least ask your family members and husband", suggested her kind boss, "I am sure they will be happy for you." "No way," she exclaimed, "I can't ask my husband or my in-laws to allow me to go away for two months."

She soon got pregnant and her family was overjoyed. She immediately resigned from her work. "You don't have to resign," her boss said, "We have a liberal maternity leave policy and I would love to have you back at work, once your baby has arrived. I will also ensure that you work flexi-time, so that you can spend more time with your child." "Oh no! I can't do that!" Anita sighed, "I can't leave my baby at home with my in-laws. I will never be able to concentrate on my work with my baby at home. " "At least speak to your husband, dear," her boss suggested, "I am sure they would not mind. Even if they did, I think you need to take this decision on your own. Millions of women go to work after their pregnancy. I know that will be difficult, but definitely not impossible for someone as talented as you. Would you like me to speak to your husband?" "Never! I can't allow you to speak to him on my behalf. He will be so hurt. And it is unfair to ask my in-laws to take care of the baby." And in spite of several of her friends and family members offering to help, Anita resigned from her job and in a few months gave birth to a healthy, beautiful daughter.

Priti, on the other hand, joined a small organization, as a junior accountant. She had already agreed to a marriage proposal from one of her seniors from college, who had relentlessly pursued her for three years, before wrangling a 'yes' from her. He was academically brilliant and had a great future in the company where he was working. And Priti had already been in love with him now for more than a year.

Their wedding was a frantic affair, because he was expected to go to Australia for a year for an important assignment. And he wanted to take Priti along. Priti, who had by now been working for a year in India, resigned from her job. Not wanting to depend on anyone for financial support, Priti took up a job as an accountant in Australia. Though the salary was a pittance, she saved enough in a couple of months to pay her fees for a Financial Management course. Her husband was very busy and tried hard to help but it was often impossible for him with his work commitments. So as is the case often, the domestic chores and cooking fell on her shoulders. Add to that her work and evening classes, her life was hectic.

The year soon got over and the couple now came back to India, just in time for Priti to apply for an MBA degree. She found a job near the institute where she had her evening classes and it was seldom that she was home before 10 pm. And then the fights started. It started with casual digs and subtle hints from her husband and in-laws. And slowly it increased to accusations and attacks on her callousness and 'so-called ambition'. Shudder! Imagine if a woman has an ambition. She tried her best to ignore the fights and one day sat them down and emphatically asserted, "I love all of you a lot. And I know that you are concerned about me. But if I did not do this, I would be very unhappy. I want to build my career and I know that given a little time, I can manage my work, studies and home a little better. It is a matter of a couple of years and I am sure you will support me in my efforts." It took a lot of effort and courage to be able to confront her family. And God knows her hands were trembling when she spoke to them. But from that day on they left her more or less alone.

During her second semester, Priti discovered that she was expecting a child. It was a moment of joy for everyone. Her husband and in-laws pampered her and went out of their way to fulfil her every desire. But she had a difficult pregnancy. She suffered from severe nausea and edema. And sometimes, her backache was so severe that it would bring tears to her eyes. Everyone advised her against continuing her job and her studies. But she was adamant, "I can do it", she said, "I can take the pain. It is normal. If I take a break now, I will never be able to rejoin – neither the college nor my job". And she gave birth to a beautiful son right after her first year examinations.

Soon after her son's birth, her father-in-law received the news that his brother had expired in their hometown and there was no one to take care of the property. Her in-laws, for several years, had anyway decided to spend the rest of their life at their ancestral home. But this tragic event expedited their process of migration. And amidst tears and kisses, they left for their hometown when the baby was barely a month old. Priti was now in a dilemma. But she was not ready to give up on her studies or her job – not yet. She spoke to her boss and explained why she didn't want to take a break in her career, "I know that if I take a break, I will lose touch with industry and it will be very difficult for me to get a job again. I know that the job market is undergoing a surge and I don't want to be left behind simply because I didn't want to push myself for a few more months." Her boss, an understanding man, saw the passion in her and offered her a part-time project for the next one year. She had to work on this project in the mornings for about four hours every day with a substantial cut in salary. But Priti was not bothered. "At the most I will have to forego a few small conveniences," she told herself, "but it will be worth it."

She found a babysitter, who was willing to take care of the baby in the mornings when she went to work and for a few hours in the evenings, while she was away attending her classes. And when the baby was three months old, a very anxious but determined Priti handed over her son to the babysitter and for the next nine months attended every work day and every lecture without a break.

It wasn't a surprise when the first year marks were announced and she had topped her batch. But now the second year was a definite challenge. "Look. You don't have to kill yourself," her husband explained to her, "Just passing is enough. I will do what I can to help you, though I can't promise too much time. My company is undergoing major expansion and I am heading several projects". "Don't worry. I can get good scores. I just need to push myself for a few months more," she assured him, "You go ahead and be the best you can be at work. I intend to be the best I can be in my academics."

She now had a grueling schedule. She would start her day at 5 am. She and her husband would do all the domestic chores before her son woke up at 6.30. She would then tend to him and spend time with him till 9.30. Then she would drop him at the baby sitter's and rush to work, where she would work till 2. She then would pick up her son and go back home where she would bathe him, feed him and get dinner ready. She would drop her son at the baby sitter's at 6. Take a bus to college, reaching at 7. Finish her lecture by 9 and rush back home by about 9.45 with her little son in tow. The second year of MBA was even more tedious than the first. She had assignments and projects and homework, which she would complete overnight with her son sleeping in her lap. She would catch up on some sleep and would be back in the kitchen at 5.

Watching her run about, there was no dearth of comments from her family, friends and most importantly, neighbours. "Ambition," they would drawl to each other, "Look how ambition has killed her maternal instincts." "She thinks she can manage everything," they would snigger. "What kind of a mother are you? Don't you love your son?" they exclaimed. "You are killing yourself. Why don't you stay home and take care of our son," her husband would point out. Priti would just continue her work, she hardly had energy for any retort.

And finally her MBA was over. She had topped her college. She soon rejoined her organization as a Senior Executive. By now, her son was slightly older and easier to manage. Her husband was awed at her strength and purpose. And her in-laws and parents were proud of her success.

Priti bumped into Anita after about 15 years at a mall. Amidst hugs and tears, they introduced their families to each other. Both of them had two children each now. And while the husbands herded the children towards the play zone, the two estranged friends caught up with each other's lives over a cup of coffee.

When Anita heard about Priti's career (she was now the Financial Controller with an MNC), she wept with tears of bitterness and envy, "I had so many opportunities. But I wasted my talent. I have no identity other than being my husband's wife and my children's mother. If I had not had any ambition, I would have been happy – like so many other women who have always wanted to be home makers. But I really wanted to have a career. I really wanted to be financially independent. And now it is too late!"

"It is never too late," Priti assured her friend, "You were always very creative. And you look like a fashionista. Why don't you do a fashion designing course? I am sure that now

that the children are grown up, you can take some time out for yourself. You are only 34." "But I can't," Anita wailed, "Your life is different. My children are just too demanding. They want me at home when they come back from school. My husband comes home for lunch and wants his food fresh and hot. And my in-laws are not at all supportive. I have no time and no energy left for anything. I can't, I just can't, yaar."

We, like Priti, have nothing more to say.

THE STORY OF TWO BUSINESS OWNERS

This story is about Amit Patel and Nimish Shah. Both were born and brought up in Mehsaana (Gujarat). Being the children of poor farmer parents, who found it difficult to make ends meet, both migrated to Mumbai – the land of dreams, the land of opportunities – when they were barely out of their teens.

They had an uncle in Mumbai, who promised them a place to sleep in and a job in his textile warehouse. Amit and Nimish were wide-eyed as they saw Mumbai for the first time. They exclaimed in fear when they saw the crowds and the traffic, the opulence and the poverty. They looked awed at the huge buildings and the dirty slums. They cried out in surprise when they were jostled and pushed by the bustle of people each trying to get to the other side of where they were. It was a riot. It was crazy. It was exhilarating.

Both Amit and Nimish merged into the veins of the city, like fish in water. They loved the hustle, the noise, the vibrancy. They were hard workers and were willing to learn and soon became an indispensable part of their uncle's business. The uncle loved these spirited young boys and it wasn't long before he was buying more warehouses. When after a few years, their uncle wanted to retire, he offered them the business to run, with the assurance that they would pay him a fixed amount every month with fixed increases every year till the day he died. Both Amit and Nimish were overjoyed. They decided to split the business exactly in half and each became now an owner of four warehouses each.

Amit and Nimish (now called Amitbhai and Nimishbhai, having proven their mettle and being business owners), took over the business seamlessly. They continued using the same name for the business – Mansukhlal Cloth Traders. They were soon known names in the textile market. They remained friends and would catch up with each other once every couple of months. Each danced the most in the other's wedding and distributed sweets to the entire neighbourhood when the other's children were born.

It was not long before the wives and the children were enmeshed as an integral part of each other's lives, celebrating festivals and weekends together, going for annual holidays together and being a part of each other's successes and failures. It was on one of these holidays that Amitbhai and Nimishbhai met a Chartered Accountant who was in the same hotel as them. When the CA came to know that they were entrepreneurs, he was curious to know more about their business. And both Amitbhai and Nimishbhai, always ready for conversation and free advice, shared their growth story with him.

The CA then advised them to convert their proprietorship into a Private Limited firm. "You will be able to grow faster because then your legal status is enhanced," he said, "In the future if you want to raise capital of apply for bank loans, private limited firms always have a better chance." "I can't," declared Nimishbhai, "Who will untangle the accounts and old records? And I know that once you are a private limited company, you will have to file for tax returns and pay taxes more religiously. I also know the audits will be more rigorous and the documentation will have to be more accurate. I can't do all that now after so many years of running the business."

Amitbhai, on the other hand, seemed deep in thought. "Can I have your visiting card?" he asked the CA, "I would like to meet you and understand this in more detail." "Arre... have you gone gaando (mad)?" Nimishbhai asked Amitbhai, "Why are you wasting time?" Amitbhai just shrugged and changed the topic.

It wasn't long before there were two companies in the textile market – Mansukhlal and Co. and Mansukhlal Textiles Pvt. Ltd. The first year, Amitbhai ended up making much lesser profits because he was too busy clearing up the mess. "You are crazy," fumed Nimishbhai, "All your competitors are laughing at you. The market is booming. All of us have made dramatic profits. And you have barely managed to break even. What is wrong with you?" Amitbhai looked at Nimishbhai for a long moment, "But these are not my competitors," he said, "My competitor is Roshani," Roshani Textiles Ltd. was a 3000 crore organization, "I am preparing myself to compete with them." Nimishbhai shook his head, "You don't know what you are talking about. Roshani is way beyond our capacity."

The next year was even worse. Amitbhai had to declare all his assets and convert his cash business to white. He had to pay pending taxes and had to let go of several of his old employees who couldn't adapt themselves to the new system. That year Nimishbhai sponsored their annual vacation. It was a grim holiday and Nimishbhai didn't let go of any opportunity to remind Amitbhai about his foolishness.

And then the market slumped.

The only business available was from corporates and the government sector – who preferred to deal with private limited organizations than with proprietary concerns. Mansukhlal Textiles Pvt. Ltd. managed to break even, while Mansukhlal and company barely scraped through.

This time it was Amitbhai who sponsored the annual holiday of both the families.

"I can't pay the annual bonus this year," said a frustrated Nimishbhai, "and I know that my purchase guy is cheating me." "Sack him," said Amitbhai, "Credibility and trust is everything." "I can't," wailed Nimishbhai, "Given the amount of cash transactions, I can't prove anything. And everything is such a mess, I can't let him go."

Amitbhai soon came to know that there was a textile manufacturing unit for sale, as the owner had suffered heavy losses and wanted to get out of the business. He approached both Nimishbhai and Amitbhai. "I can't buy this company," emphasized Nimishbhai, "What is the guarantee that I can turn it around? I may be able to raise the capital, but taking over a factory that I don't know anything about... that's too much risk." Amitbhai just shrugged and said, "I can raise the capital and buy the factory. I think it makes good business sense." Within a few months, Amitbhai, who had raised the money through bank finance, was not only trading in textiles, but was also manufacturing grey material for selling to companies who were in the business of cloth manufacturing.

And then the government regulations changed. And Mansukhlal and company had to face the most rigorous audit that they had ever faced. "Improve your accounting and inventory management system," admonished the auditor kindly, "that's the only way you and other companies like yours will survive in the long run." "I can't," wailed Nimishbhai, "I can't try to systematize my company now. There is too much of a mess." Amitbhai at this stage, had already appointed two consultants to systematize his inventory systems and his HR systems. His turnover was now close to 200 crores, what with the acquisition of the factory and the regular orders from both corporate and government tenders.

While Nimishbhai found himself more and more entwined in sorting his daily operations, having to keep a close watch on every activity, Amitbhai now had a team of qualified people who were managing the independent functions and departments professionally. "Recruit a good team," Amitbhai advised Nimishbhai. "I can't," justified Nimishbhai, "they charge a bomb and I don't have the wherewithal to manage them." "Then learn the technique of managing people who are more qualified than you," said Amitbhai, who by now was actively involved in several entrepreneurial study groups and had recently attended a course on Management. "I can't," retorted Nimishbhai. "It is too late. I am too old to learn. I can't sit in a classroom and learn new things now."

Textech was one of the most prestigious textile exhibitions in the world. And Amitbhai invited Nimishbhai to participate in it, "Come na, yaar. The market abroad is open to importing textiles from India. I will route all my exports through you. Just take a stall this year. The exhibition is in Germany. I am sure you will find enough customers abroad." "I can't, simply can't," whined Nimishbhai. "What? Stand there and talk to foreigners in English about my range of products? I will look like a fool. I can't even speak in English."

Suffice to share that today, 15 years later, Mansukhlal Textiles Pvt. Ltd. is a ₹2500 crore company and Roshani Ltd.

has strategic meetings almost every day to determine newer approaches to recovering their market share. Amitbhai now takes his family abroad for vacations several times and year and never forgets to invite Nimishbhai, who declines.

THE STORIES – DECODED

'I can't' is a powerful excuse for most of us. It helps us to stay in our comfort zones. It helps us to stay safe, secure, protected from the unknown. It keeps us from starting something whose outcomes are not definite. People's biggest fear is that if they explore the unknown, the un-done, the uninitiated, the unconventional, the new, the different, they will look like fools not realizing that they are actually fools for not grabbing the opportunity to do exactly that.

When one says, 'I can't' in the beginning, it sounds defensive. The 'can't' doesn't sound totally justified, at least not yet. But it sounds worth a few words of resistance. And the seed has been sown. A few more times of 'I can't' makes the belief stronger. And repeating it often enough makes it the truth – Your truth. This play of thoughts on the mind is called Perception. Perception is a very potent attitude towards the world, people and circumstances. It is those assumed (and in most cases unreasoned) beliefs that determine the way we live our entire life.

There is a Hindi movie titled "404 – Error not found". It is one of the most intriguing movies on perception that you will ever see (we loved it). It is the story of a student, Abhimanyu, who is a fresher in one of the most prestigious medical colleges in the country. He is handsome, suave, dashing and very bright. He is academically brilliant and completely 'all there'. He and his friends, like all other freshers, are subjected to ragging by their seniors. He takes it sportingly for several days, but when it becomes a little too humiliating and vicious, he complains to the warden of the hostel. And you can imagine how the circumstances change after that. The seniors are reprimanded and warned. That only gives them more impetus to rag the juniors even more maliciously – especially Abhimanyu and his roommates.

There is one particularly disturbing incident when the boys find their hostel room and beds strewn with blood and entrails from the morgue. His roommates verbally abuse Abhimanyu because they are convinced that if he hadn't complained, they would have been spared and left alone like the other freshers were. Abhimanyu offers to shift his room. But there are no rooms available, hostels being over-occupied anyway in most residential colleges across the country. But he has noticed that a room on the 4th floor – 404 – is locked. And he approaches the warden to be shifted to that room. The warden refuses outright. "We can't give that room to anyone," he explains to Abhimanyu, "A fresher, Gaurav, committed suicide by hanging himself from the ceiling fan two years back. And we don't think it is a good omen to allot that room to anyone." But Abhimanyu is adamant. He approaches the Principal and then the Director and argues, "We are medical students. We believe in science and work on research. We thrive on logic and analysis. It is a ridiculous notion that a room where a poor student has died cannot be occupied because of "bad luck" and "ill omen". I am not afraid to stay in that room. I don't believe in ghosts and I insist that you allot the room to me. It is anyway vacant and there is no harm to giving it someone." And in spite of severe resistance and discouragement from every one, except one professor, who is the Head of Department (HOD) for Psychiatry, he gets the room.

Abhimanyu is happy to get the room all to himself. He now has enough space for his books, gear, clothes and most importantly, he does not have to queue up for the toilet any more. He settles into his new room, when one evening, as he is tying his show-laces just near the door, he hears someone banging on his door. He opens it only to find that there is no one outside – not outside his door and not in the entire corridor. He just assumes that the banging must have been on some other door and proceeds for dinner. About a couple of days later, he is about to leave his room again. He switches off the room lights and locks the door. He sees the ward boy changing a bulb some distance away and complains to him about some trivial infrastructure issue. The ward boy retorts, "At least switch off your room lights before complaining." "But I did," says Abhimanyu and turns towards his room, only to find that light is spilling from his room from the ventilator above his door. "Sir, be careful. Many funny things have been going on in that room," warns the ward boy before scampering off. A confused Abhimanyu opens the door, switches off the lights (yet again?) and continues on his way out.

A few days later, the wall-mounted phone at the end of the corridor rings insistently. Seeing no one around to answer it, he does. There is a voice from the other end. "What are you doing in my room? I am Gaurav and that room belongs to me," the voice hisses into the phone. A distressed Abhimanyu calls out to the ward boy and demands that the authorities do something about the silly pranks that are being played on him. He tells the ward boy about the phone call and insists on knowing who has access to the number. The ward boy stares at him and stutters, "But that phone has been dead for over six months. It didn't ring. Or else I would have heard it." "But it did ring. See?" Abhimanyu picks up the receiver to prove his point and realizes that the phone is actually dead.

Small incidents like this keep happening. One day, Abhimanyu is knocked unconscious outside his room. And when he wakes up, he is in complete darkness, unable to move. All he can feel is a presence around him and hear strange malicious voices, "I am Gaurav," "That room is mine," "Get out of that room," "The bed that you sleep in is mine," "The table where you keep your books, I used to study there," "Get out," "Go away," "Can't you see my dead body hanging from the fan?"… and on and on for time that seems indefinite and suspended, for hours, eons, minutes.

When Abhimanyu gains consciousness, he finds himself on the floor outside his room. He staggers up into his room and screams falling back on the floor as he sees Gaurav's dead body hanging from the ceiling fan. He stumbles towards the wash basin to wash his face and when he looks up into the mirror, he finds Gaurav standing behind him, staring at him. When he pushes his way out of the bathroom and falls on his bed, he sees Gaurav sitting at the study table staring at him.

In the next few days, Gaurav seems to be everywhere. Sharing the desk in the class with Abhimanyu. Sitting at the same table as Abhimanyu in the canteen. Behind toilet doors. Beside him in the library. Abhimanyu, now a terrified wreck, barges into the Principal's cabin and confesses, "You were right, sir. Gaurav's ghost is in that room. I can see him." And despite his friends, professors, the Principal, everyone convincing him otherwise, he now firmly believes in Gaurav's ghost inhabiting the premises. He spends his days talking to Gaurav. He misses all his classes. The once brilliant student is now a lost, crazed neurotic. He is unstable, psychologically affected. And now a nervous wreck of complexes and perceptions.

The movie takes a very interesting turn. And we don't want to kill the suspense for you. So, go ahead and watch it.

That's the power of perception. Once a perception is programmed in your mind, it cannot be removed. It is like Gaurav, who will make his presence felt in everything you do or want to do. And if you repeat the thought often enough to yourself and if there are people around you who can echo that same thought, it becomes 'your' truth and Gaurav becomes 'real'. Every time you said, "I can't", you will find a hundred others who will convince you that you can't.

"I can't take part in the marathon, yaar," you will say. "You are right. Look at us. We are past our prime," people around you will agree.

• • •

"I can't leave my kids with a babysitter and restart my career," you will wail. "You are right. Babysitters are not to be trusted. I heard of a terrible incident about how a babysitter tortured my friend's child," your friend will nod dramatically.

• • •

"I can't insist on cheque payments from my clients," you will claim. "Of course we can't. This can't happen in our business. These consultants know nothing," your co-trader will shake his head ruefully.

• • •

"I can't learn English now at this age," you will confess. "You are right. One needs to be from an English Medium School for their English to be perfect. And it is too late for us," your co-director will nod his head sagely.

• • •

The list is endless.

But what happened in the stories was an eye-opener for most of you, we are guessing. For every 'I can't', there is an equal opportunity for 'I can'. It is about making a choice at that precise moment when your 'can't' peeps out. It is about pulling the 'can' out and using that as a shield.

You know too many inspiring stories to be disillusioned by what we are saying. You know too many people who have succeeded to be disbelieving. You know too many motivating incidents to be sceptical. Now is the time to replace your 'I can't' with 'I can'.

All the best.

BREAK FREE TRUTH 5

I can.

BREAK FREE TRUTH 5 - IN A 'KICK-ASS' FORMAT

'I can't', 'I can't', 'I can't'... done with it? Or do you need some more chucks on your head? Did you know that you have been saying "I can't" to so many things that people have nicknamed you with the same prefix. So, when you pass by on the street, they point out to you say, "Oye! There goes I-can't-Sapan-Banerjee." Or when you are in the supermarket, your friend introduces you to her husband with, "Hellooooooo! This is my dear friend I-can't-Pramila-Gandhi." Or when you walk into your office, your subordinates whisper to each other, "Here he is. I-can't-Mangesh-Borkar." And every time your boss has to call you for a project he tells the office boy, "Can you send I-can't-Vinod-Nair to my cabin?"

Hee! Hee! That was really funny. Stop laughing, I-can't-Ashok-Pandey.

But the worst part is, you can't bear to see someone else saying 'I can'. You then go out of your way to prove to the other person why he can't either. You will use scary, mindless, thoughtless, stories to put the fear of God into those who even want to try. And your lame (yes, very lame) excuse is that you care and you are concerned and are afraid that he will fail.

NO! The truth is you are afraid that he will not. You are afraid that he will prove you wrong. You are terrified that he will succeed. You are afraid that you will not have company when you start your 'I can't' whining. Shame on you!

If you really don't want to do something, have the guts to say "I am too scared to do it." JUST SAY IT. And feel the difference. Because owning up to your lack of courage, perversely, takes more courage.

If you don't have the gall (read balls) to do something new, or different, at least don't discourage others. If you can't motivate yourself at least take on the role of motivating others. Or else, we all know what your eulogy will read, "Here lies the man whose name I forget, but we used to lovingly call him 'I can't' and also 'You can't' by the one's closest to him. He was a worrier (not warrior) when he was young. And he didn't change much till the day he died. We will miss his dejected face and his dispirited comments."

And they will all proceed to sing his favourite song in his memory *Saari duniya ka bojh hum uthate hain*.

So… Go on to the next page which has the 5 BREAK FREE TRUTHS TRACKER. And for God's sake, don't say 'I can't'. All the best.

THE 5 BREAK FREE TRUTHS TRACKER – WEEK 5

Your Truth – I can't.
The Truth – I can.

What I Believed – My Truth	*I have always wanted to speak in public. And whenever I got the opportunity I just shook my head sadly and said 'I can't'. So many chances lost to do something that I have always wanted to do.*
What The Truth Is – My Realizations	*I have been using the shield of 'I can't' very effectively. It has kept me afraid and secure throughout my life. The truth is I have been gutless and spineless. I was terrified to even try because I was afraid that I will look like a fool. My realization is that I am bigger fool for not even trying.*

My Next Step	*I am going enrol for Public Speaking Classes. I am going to look for opportunities to speak in front of an audience. I am going to take feedback and criticism sportingly and learn from my mistakes. And I will never discourage others either.*
My Truth Partner	Vijaya Suvarna (Empowerment Coach)

THE 5 BREAK FREE TRUTHS TRACKER – WEEK 5

Your Truth – I can't.
The Truth – I can

What I Believed – 'My' Truth	
What The Truth Is – My Realizations	
My Next Step	
My Truth Partner	

HOW OTHERS AROUND YOU HAVE DISCOVERED THIS TRUTH

An experience shared by Amol will take us a long way in understanding how others have discovered this truth.

'This was in the January of 2010. We were training the officers of Uttar Pradesh Rajya Vidyut Utpadan Nigam Ltd. (UPRVUNL), a state-owned company managed by the U.P. State Electricity Board. The 10,000 member-strong organization was led by a dynamic IAS officer who felt the need to bring about an attitudinal change in the organization given the enhanced expectations of the citizens. So, we had designed a three day training module on change and change management titled Parivartan to be conducted at all the power stations of UPRVUNL. I facilitated the first day on 'change and how it was affecting the power sector', Dr. Khanvte facilitated the second day on "self-motivation and change", while Mr. Rajesh Tagore facilitated the third day on breaking the paradigms. We were housed at a power station on the outskirts of Kanpur. On the third day of training workshop, the three of us went for a morning jog at 5 am to a large ground nearby.

As we started running together and completed a few laps, the then 61-year-old Dr. Khanvte and the 42-year-old Tagore went past ahead of me, and that too with so much of ease, as if they were on a pleasure walk. I fell hopelessly behind. Not a motivating situation; I was 31, much younger than both of them! After a few more laps of panting and pulling myself along, I just stood aside watching helplessly as the two "oldies" completed lap after lap and were encouraging me to run. On the way back, while I was comparing my poor stamina with theirs, Dr. Khanvte asked, "Amol, you're running the marathon this year?" I said, "Yeah, I'm thinking of registering for the half marathon." At this point, Tagore asked "Why half?" I said "Well… because the full-marathon is 42 kilometres and I've never run that much. I can't. Even the half-marathon of 21 kilometres is going to be a big challenge for me!" Not satisfied with this reply, Tagore asked "But, why can't you? If you can run 21 kilometres, you might as well try for 42 kilometres. Can't you?"

I had no answer to his, "Why can't you?" I tried very hard searching for an excuse, but couldn't find one. That year I ran the first marathon of my life, the Standard Chartered Mumbai Marathon. I was probably the slowest. Didn't even get a medal as the deadline to finish the 42 kilometres was 6 hours; I took 7 hours 38 minutes. No one to cheer, no one to applaud, no photographers to click the momentous event! Even the organizers had left by the time I reached the finishing line (for all my friends, I have been a butt of jokes for this one; they can't stop laughing imagining the scene! Yeah it's funny!). But only I know the pride I felt and the joy I experienced on finishing the gruelling run! It had turned my 'I can't' to 'I can'!'

What Mr. Rajesh Tagore and Dr. Khanvte did was they acted as the "I-Can-Triggers" for Amol. "I-Can-Triggers" are those people who challenge us. They are those who come up with uncomfortable questions like "why can't you?" Everyone has "I-Can-Triggers" around them. These might be your near and dear ones, your wife, your daughter, your father, your boss, your sports coach, your business partner or a professional business coach appointed by you – anyone who has seen the potential in you. These are people who truly want you to succeed and therefore challenge you with questions that you find uncomfortable to answer.

⌐

Mr. Darshan Mevada and Mr. Hitesh Mevada of NKP Pharma Machineries Pvt. Ltd., a super-ambitious organization based in Ahmedabad faced a peculiar situation in 2007. The company manufactures and supplies large machineries for the *pharmaceutical industry. While the entire pharmaceutical industry was going through a slowdown, the demand for machinery in the domestic market dropped radically. Their challenge was to maintain their growth rate in spite of the slump. The only viable option was to increase the focus on exports and generate business from countries that were hitherto unexplored. The brothers were ready to take up the challenge, but it wasn't the market that was tough, it was convincing their own team that was the real challenge.*

'We can't compete with German quality, they are simply too good for us.' 'We don't have standard designs for our machines. With so much customization we cannot multiply the production.' 'We are unable to provide timely post-installation service to our domestic clients as we don't have a customer service team. All we do is pull out our best production supervisors to handle service-calls. Imagine our plight when the extremely demanding clients from U.S. and Europe place orders with us!' 'We can't cope up with the tight deadlines the overseas clients expect us to work on.' Statements like these and more did the rounds in the conference room when the HODs were meeting for the umpteenth time to discuss the next course of action.

The brothers only retaliated with 'Why can't we?' till the HODs ran out of excuses. With each new 'We can't' their resolve for 'We can' became stronger.

Mr. Darshan Mevada took charge of the front-end, visiting several new countries, touring twenty to twenty five days a month. Having identified several new clients, he negotiated heavily on the lead time. It was a win-win for the overseas customers as the Indian machines came for one-third the price the Germans were offering. A few extra days of wait was worth the price difference for them. Some clients even went to the extent of replacing entire German production lines with the ones from NKP Pharma. Surprisingly, as the export orders poured in, the sales team handling domestic market led by Ashish Nair felt a renewed sense of energy and were able to crack several significant orders.

Mr. Hitesh Mevada took charge of the back-end, systematizing the entire design process, documenting each and every step and allotting codes to more than ten thousand parts that went into the making of a single machine. A young and dynamic design expert, Alpesh Mistry was handed over the charge of this process and designated GM – R&D. Mr. Hitesh Mevada also set up a dedicated customer service team under the leadership of Nilesh – a seasoned production supervisor who had hands-on experience of providing customer service. He was designated as the new customer service manager.

That left the GM –Production, Deepak Thotawalla, with only one task to worry about – Quality production within the set deadline. And he and his team delivered.

The results soon became visible. While all other machinery manufacturers were struggling, NKP Pharma grew by 40 percent that year. In fact, the demand rose to such an extent that the existing factory couldn't cope. They had to buy the adjacent plot of land where a new building was erected within months. Support departments like electrical, electronics, design and development and quality Check were shifted to this new building and production and assembly got the entire factory to themselves. Needless to say, NKP Pharma has been growing every year while several other machinery manufacturers are struggling for survival. The story of NKP Pharma is now an inspiration to hundreds of other engineering companies who are stuck with their 'I can't'.

You might have seen in the previous pages that the 'I-can-trigger' can be a person close to you, who cares for you and whose words you respect or you can be the trigger yourself. While we were the Business Coaches to the Mevada brothers, and played the 'I-can-trigger' several times, it was they who acted as the 'I-can-trigger' for their team.

FACING THIS TRUTH RIGHT NOW

'I can't' is a lie that all of us have uttered a hundred times about a hundred different things. It's an all-pervading lie! The most ordinary men have lived this lie and so have even the most successful people!

Let's now build upon what we have discussed so far. While fighting the lie 'I can't', we need to focus simultaneously on two things–

1. Identifying and developing 'I-can' triggers around you.
2. Becoming an 'I-can' trigger for others around you.

We will now use the shorter version – 'trigger' for 'I-can' trigger to make matters simple.

1. Identifying and developing Triggers around you:

All of us have dreams and all of us have at some point or the other have shared them with others. Every time we share dreams that are large and gigantic, the fear within is that the other person will laugh, will make fun of us. And yes, some of our friends actually do laugh, and yes, they will make fun of us!

In our case too, our gigantic dreams have met with cynicism – '*Aaj lagta hai subah subah pee lee hai sahab ne*' (looks like my lord is quite drunk early in the morning!), with concern '*Aapki tabiyat to theek hai?'* (Are you feeling alright?). And even outright criticism *'Chehra dekha hai aainey mein?'* (Have you looked at yourself in the mirror, dude?)

But there is definitely this person in your life (or more than one person in many cases) who doesn't laugh at you, who doesn't seem shocked, and who doesn't react with disbelief. In fact, he/she appears perfectly at ease with the thought and probably encourages you to go ahead and do it. Their eyes shine brightly on hearing your dream, they incite confidence in you with their, 'Of course you were destined to do this. Go ahead!' These are the people who have asked you sometime or the other in life 'Why can't you?'

We have had several people like them in our life who have asked us 'Why can't you?' These are the people we call Triggers. We are sure you have your own Triggers too. It is impossible to live in a society and not have at least one Trigger around you. Simply impossible! The only case where it is possible to be not surrounded with Triggers is if you have been meditating on the top of Mount Kailash for the past forty years and have already attained Nirvana! Or in the case where you are already dead! Since we assume, none of the above has happened to you, we can safely conclude that you have in your life a few Triggers.

We have already discussed how you can identify the Triggers. Let's now discuss how we can develop more of such people in our life.

A. Define Your Vision - The legendary Dr. Steven Covey, in his book *The 8ᵗʰ Habit* (which is a sequel to his best-selling *7 Habits of Highly Effective People*) writes about vision –

Vision is seeing a future state with the mind's eye. Vision is applied imagination. All things are created twice; first, a mental creation, second, a physical creation. The first creation, vision, is the beginning of the process of reinventing oneself or of an organization reinventing itself. It represents desires, dreams, hopes, goals and plans. But these dreams or visions are not just fantasies. They are reality not yet brought into the physical sphere, like the blueprint of a house before it's built or musical notes in a score just waiting to be played.

It is therefore everyone's responsibility to define his/her vision. However, unless this vision is shared with others, the probability of it coming to reality remains pretty low. Both of us have been making 'vision posters' every year for the past eleven years. Every year, we make our 'vision posters' and display them at prominent places in our home where we can see them regularly. We also share a lot of our goals with our family members, colleagues, co-professionals, clients and even the participants of our training workshops at large. The reason? While we get cynics in large numbers in every audience, there's at least one in the audience who believes in us. Imagine the number of Triggers we are surrounded with. They are the ones who energize us, remind us of our commitments, write to us, applaud us on our small victories and even share their stories of success. It's fun to be surrounded by the Triggers.

Remember, the more people you share your dreams with, the more Triggers you will develop. So, write down your dreams today and share them with as many people you can. And if you share it with 100 people, you will get one Trigger. Any better proportion than this, and you can consider yourself extremely lucky!

B. Seek Professional Help – As said earlier, Triggers are the people who energize you to aim for big goals in life. But, they might not be the ones to enable and empower you to achieve those goals in life.

Mr. Tagore was a Trigger for Amol energizing him to run the marathon. Amol then appointed a running coach to help him learn the techniques of long-distance running. Dr. Khanvte and Mr. Tagore too kept supporting him through regular tips and books on long-distance running. *Energizing needs to be coupled with enabling and empowerment.*

In 2008, we had leased out an office space from a very fine human being and a successful business-owner himself, Mr. Rajul Shah. As our lease-term expired, we approached him for continuing with the lease. "I'll be more than happy continuing with you. But, why are you not buying your own office now? It will build your asset base and help your business," said Rajulbhai. Our immediate reaction was, "No, we can't. It's not even two years since we started our business and we can't take such a big risk." Rajulbhai played the trigger, "Why can't you? You people are hard-working and I can see that you are growing pretty well. With proper planning, you can make this happen!" He didn't stop at playing the Trigger, but guided us along the entire process. We also were ably guided by a very dynamic and committed finance consultant, Mr. Vinod Verma. He took care of the entire paperwork and ensured our involvement was to the minimum. We were able to focus on bringing money while he was managing the back-end. Thus, at a very nascent stage of operations, we were able to purchase our first office. Energizing needs to be coupled with enabling and empowerment.

⌒

A client of ours, say one Mr. Harihar Shetty, who runs a successful manufacturing plant, was faced with a peculiar problem. His plant had 150 workers and being a family managed business, he had a good equation with nearly all of them. Workers had a strong sense of belonging to the factory and the owner too treated them like his family members. Whenever they needed any help, in most cases financial help,

Mr. Shetty would generously give them loans. Such loans were treated as salary advances and were given to anyone in need without any interest charged on them. This loan was then deducted in EMIs (Equal Monthly Instalments) as jointly decided by the worker and the accounts manager. People took loans for marriages in family, for repairing homes, for children's education or for medical emergencies. While all the reasons appeared genuine, there was no way of ascertaining the truthfulness of the purpose for which the loan was availed.

As the system continued for several years, it gave rise to a peculiar issue. Many workers had too much loan pending and were yet applying for more. Some had availed of so many loans that even if they worked for salary without ten years straight, they would still fail to repay the amount. Mr. Shetty agreed that the situation was hurting the company. But, more than that he was worried about his workers! He knew for a fact that the workers were caught in the vicious trap of loans-expenses-loans and that he had aided that hazardous habit. "I can't refuse them now," said Mr. Shetty. "Why can't you?" we played the Trigger. Having convinced him on the need to set a policy that governs loans and salary advances, we proceeded to design the policy. After dozens of meetings and tearing up of several rough drafts, the policy was finally ready.

We designed the entire HRM policy document that not only covered the loans policy, but also policies pertaining to recruitment, induction and orientation, workers' training and development, travel reimbursement, cell-phone reimbursements, performance appraisal policy, organizational discipline and several others totalling to 28 key policies that were critical for the smooth functioning of Mr. Shetty's organization. The final document was approved by Mr. Shetty. It was decided that the communication of the new HRM policies were left to us as we are the HRM experts and have already defined and successfully implemented HRM policies in more than 150 companies. We decided to do so during our next visit to the plant.

Between the finalization of the HRM policies and our pending visit to the plant, Mr. Shetty handed over the policy document to his accounts manager to read. Within twenty four hours, the peaceful plant had turned into a battlefield. A production supervisor approached the accounts manager for an advance against salary. The accounts manager refused and said, "No more advances against salaries; that's an order from the management!" Within hours, the entire workforce was standing outside the plant refusing to work unless the "order" was repealed. Mr. Shetty refused to budge unless the workers weren't back on their machines. It took a lot of coaxing and cajoling on our part with both the parties to resolve the deadlock. The highly energized accounts manager cost the organization a loss of seven days of production before things could be brought back to normal!

Energizing needs to be coupled with enabling and empowerment.

2. Becoming an 'I-can' trigger for others around you

What do you do when you receive lots of blessings and are on your way to success? You bless others who are on the way to success! What do you do when you make a lot of money? You share it with the needy! So what do you do when you have developed several Triggers around? You become a Trigger for several in search of one!

Paul Hersey and Kenneth Blanchard, the ultimate authorities on scientific organization management, in their classic, *Management of Organizational Behaviour* have segregated management skill in the following three categories

Technical Skill – *Ability to use knowledge, methods, techniques and equipment necessary for the performance of specific tasks.*

Human Skill – *Ability and judgment in working with and through people, including an understanding of motivation and an application of effective leadership.*

Conceptual Skill – *Ability to understand the complexities of the overall organization and where one's own operation fits into the organization.'*

While discussing which skills are necessary to be effective at various levels in an organization, Hersey and Blanchard make the following point–

> *To be effective, less technical skill tends to be needed as one advances from lower to higher levels in the organization, but more conceptual skill is necessary. Supervisors at lower levels need considerable technical skill because they are often required to train and develop technicians and other employees in their sections. At the other extreme, executives in a business organization do not need to know how to perform all the specific tasks at the operational level. However, they should be able to see how all these functions are interrelated in accomplishing the goals of the total organization. While the amount of technical and conceptual skills needed at these different levels of management varies, the common denominator that appears to be crucial at all levels is human skill.*

This emphasis on human skill is not a thing of today. Human skills have always been important for success! Whether you are an executive working in a corporate company, or a government official handling public affairs, or a police officer stationed in a notorious area, or a student, or a homemaker, or a political leader or a business owner trying to make it big, or an artist of any kind, you need superb human skills to succeed in your field! And if that's true, then being a Trigger in the lives of people around you is just the right way to build on your human skills.

Dr. Steven Covey makes an interesting point in *The 8th Habit*–

Cultivating the habit of affirming people, of frequently and sincerely communicating your belief in them is supremely important. It's a relatively small investment with incalculable, unbelievable results. Again, remember the incredible effect it has upon us when someone communicates his or her belief in us (our potential) when we don't believe in ourselves (our history).

It is not just our duty, but also a privilege to play the Trigger in someone else's life. The rewards of playing a Trigger in someone's life are just too many. The joy of having touched someone's life meaningfully and the honour of having helped someone to realize their true potential is absolutely indescribable. Believe us, it is a feeling that can only be experienced, not described. We have played the Trigger for hundreds of people and we consider ourselves very lucky that they allowed us to contribute to their lives. The feeling is terrific! Try it!

But, don't stop at energizing people to achieve their dreams. Go one step ahead; help them develop the ability to accomplish those dreams. Recommend books to them, or training workshops, or suggest professional sports coaches, or business coaches or experts in the area that they are trying to excel in. You can ask them thought and action-provoking questions like–

- Would you like to convert all your 'I-can't' to 'I-can'?
- Would you like to try out all those things you have never dared to try?
- Would you like to be surrounded by Triggers around you?
- Would you like to become a Trigger for people around you?
- Would you like to see your vision becoming a reality?

Suffice it to say, that even your best intentions (triggers) are not going to make everyone achieve everything. Don't let that affect you. Remember – Your Life's Remote Control belongs to you.

LIVING THE TRUTH RIGHT NOW

This is going to be the weirdest exercise you have ever done. But, do you must! Follow the steps... just follow the steps!

1. Take a blank sheet of paper and a pen.
2. Write down all your beliefs (or at least those that you had before you began this chapter) starting with 'I can't'. You can select from the ones mentioned at the beginning of the section or come up with your own.
3. Once you finish writing all your 'I can't's, stand in the centre of the room with the paper in your hand.
4. Now quickly start tearing it... yes tear it into as many pieces as you can – tiny, tiny, tiny pieces.
5. Now scream out aloud, 'you are dead, you are dead, you are dead' and trample on all the pieces, remember each and every piece! Let no piece go alive! Be cruel... very cruel! Keep trampling, keep screaming 'You are dead!'
6. Done? Ok. Relax. Now take a deep breath. You see, 'I can't' is dead! Well, dead people must be mourned! So, in memory of the late 'I can't', please maintain a two-minute silence. Pray that 'I can't' rest in peace! Don't laugh! Just do it!
7. 'I can't' is officially dead! Now on the next page, write all the beliefs again that you had written on the page before tearing. Just that, this time each of your sentences must begin with 'I can', 'I will' and 'I must'.

Let's consider that 'I can't' was your best friend. He was there for you in all the challenges of your life. That's how, whenever a challenge was thrown at you, instead of you responding, your dearest friend 'I can't' responded! And the words came out – 'I can't dance', 'I can't sing', 'I can't run', 'I can't multiply my business', and so on and so forth.

Now your best friend is no more! When our best friends die, we take care of their family. Don't we? 'I can't' has left his three kids behind – 'I can', 'I will' and 'I must'. They're young, but they will serve you as loyally as their father! So, every time you are faced with a challenge, you must now start the response with 'I can', 'I will' and 'I must' (remember... your friend 'I can't' is no more!).

Go ahead! What are you waiting for? Feel the power flowing through your veins once you do all the steps in the exercise. Or you can call in your Truth Partner or assemble your Truth Group together to do the exercise jointly. It will be fun. But whatever you do, you must do it right now! Yes, right now!

Trust us. If you don't do this right now, this moment lost will be lost forever! Don't bother if family members are looking at you askance! Don't worry about their sniggers and rude comments. It was not their lie and it doesn't matter to them whether you have just uncovered 'The Truth' that is about to change your life! In fact, you must do ALL the steps just because they are watching!

Come on... get up! Get going!

The 7th Step
(Only *after* You Have Completed the First Six Steps)

Sr. No.	*Now Write Down Your Truth Statements....*
	I CAN / I WILL / I MUST

I CAN / I WILL / I MUST
I CAN / I WILL / I MUST
I CAN / I WILL / I MUST

Oho! So you thought it was over? Nah! Not yet.
Picture abhi baaki hai, mere dost.
(The show ain't over, my friend)

We thought we should give you one more Bonus Truth. Don't worry. We haven't charged you for this. This is under the special introductory scheme – buy 5 and get 1 free offer. This is the *baap (father)* of all Truths. The one you will be tempted to say after you have read all the others. The one that will decide whether you will consciously live The Truths or just be happy to have read that nice new book by those nice people Vijaya and Amol.

6

Your Truth

6

I am too Insignificant to make a Difference

How can a small man like me make a difference?
There is something wrong with the system.
How can the action of one man make a difference?
I am a small fish in the big ocean.
My business is too small. So if I deal in cash, it hardly makes a big
*   difference.*
Thousands of crores stuck in scams, and you will point your finger
*   at me.*
Why don't you change the government first, then come to me?
So what if I change? Or not change? Who is noticing anyway?
One person can't change the system.
One has to follow the system.

I keep my neighbourhood clean since the *swachchtaa abhiyaan* drive, but don't expect me to clean up my organizational accounts and cash transactions. I am too small a businessman to bother about things like that.

These philosophies can only be lived by truly great people. And I am not. I am humble enough to accept that.

Why go to all that trouble, when no one going to notice anyway?

These will be the ones who don't have the conviction that they can change the world. The ones who have low self-esteem and have no doubt that given the larger scheme of things, their own small contribution will not make a big dent in the system. These are the ones who love reading and hearing about inspiring stories, but have no intention of becoming one themselves.

They think that no one is watching them, while they live a life of untruths and semi-truths. They are sure that no one is noticing their decisions, their philosophies, their attitudes, their indifference, their denial, their head-in-the-sand behaviour. These are the ones who have no intention of living any of the Five Break Free Truths because… they truly believe that they are not being watched and their being one way or the other hardly makes a difference.

No… there are no realization formats for this one. Nor are there any stories. But there are some letters that have been crafted with a lot of love and humility. These are letter that you would love to send and receive. And we really hope that you do.

So… Here is the ULTIMATE Truth.

THE TRUTH 6

Each one of us can make a significant difference.

Letter to Boss

Dear Sir,

Though I have never told you this, you will always be my hero.

I wish I had your dynamism, your discipline and your exceptionally high ethical standards. I love it when you put a firm hand on my shoulder and tell me that I can. I feel happy when you are in a great mood and anxious when you are not. I will always be grateful to you for giving me a means of livelihood.

I have seen the way you struggle to ensure that not a single month goes by without our salaries being paid. Your strength awes me.

What I admire about you is your immense patience to teach me, to guide me and your insistence that I be trained so that I can learn and grow as an individual and as a professional.

I was a very insignificant person when I joined you. But today, I have a status amongst my friends and family members. I speak better, I dress better, I work better. I owe my confidence and competence to you.

I have worked with other bosses, but believe me when I say that you are the best. As I rise up the organizational ladder, I want to be just like you – strong but kind, dynamic but patient, intelligent but humble. Thank you for being there for me.

Yours Sincerely,
Santosh

Letter to Brother

Dear Bhaiya (Brother),

Though I have never told you this, you will always be my hero.

I admire the way you have taken on the responsibility of not only your wife's family, but also ours. I know managing the tempers of two different families can't be easy. Believe me, I still haven't figured that one out yet.

My best memories from childhood are eagerly waiting for you to come back from school, so that I can follow you around. I still remember that you used to bully me a lot and make me cry. But I also remember that you were my staunchest supporter and that you have had to face the anger of both Mummy and Papa on several occasions because of me.

I know that you used to save even the smallest of gifts or the tiniest of sweets for me. Others have two parents and I am lucky to have three.

I am yet to learn how you manage to retain your good humor in the midst of crisis. I know that I can count on you for tough but loving guidance. You are the best brother in the world.

Though I have never told you this, you are and always will be my hero.

Your brother,
Sanjay

Letter to Mother

Dear Mummy,

I have never told you this. But you will always be my hero.

I know that you have had a tough life despite which you have reached a pinnacle that most women just dream of. It must have taken you tremendous hard work and sacrifice to be the kind of woman you are today. It is not every woman who can have the strength to be a role model to other women. And I know that you are to hundreds of them – our family, friends, neighbors.

In a society where it is difficult for women to make their mark and stand up to what one believes in, you have amazed me with your persistence, patience, passion and purpose. Seems like all my cares just melt away when I lie with my head in your lap. I love it when you serve me food made with your own hands, rub oil in my head, go shopping with me and surprise me with silly gifts. I know that as long as you are around, I will never lack for food or love.

I thank you for having brought me into this world and setting me such a fine example. My greatest pleasure is when someone tells me that I am exactly like you. Even when I am away, I don't miss you, because I am a part of you and you are inside me – your words, your advice, your laughter, your thoughts, your love.

Though I have never told you this, you will always be my hero.

Always your little one,
Tapasya

Letter to Father

Dear Papa,

Though I have never told you this, you will always be my hero.

I wish I had your strength of purpose. I wish I had your touch of faith. I wish I had your heart of gold.

I get tears in my eyes when I think of how you've struggled your entire life. I know that you sacrificed a lot of small pleasures to ensure that your children get a good education and there is enough food on our plates every day. I remember that however tough the circumstances, you have always made sure that we celebrate our birthdays, festivals and every small accomplishment. I now realize how difficult that must have been.

You inspire me with your ability to forgive and forget. Your ability to build life-long relationships surprises me. And your ability to not show any of your pain awes me.

I love it when you put a firm hand on my shoulder and tell me that I can, and that you are always with me. You are the grandest of all men on earth and greater than all the men I know. When I grow up, I want to be just like you.

I want you to be proud of me, just as I am so proud of you. Though I have never told you this, you will always be my hero.

Your Loving Son
Amol

These are not letters of fabrication. These are real letters that we know that you would like to send and receive over and over again. These are true confessions of gratitude, words that have the power to move us and inspire us to live a life of The Ultimate Truth – that I can make a difference.

Some express their gratitude through gestures – hugs, kisses, gifts and some with words – notes, letters, phone calls, but the vast majority don't express it either way. Because criticism is so much simpler than appreciation and genuine gratitude. 'My wife is very negative' comes out so many times from our mouth pretty seamlessly, but, 'My wife is the most important person in my life' only comes out when we're cornered.

You will never know how many people take inspiration from you. The reason? Look at yourself! You take inspiration from so many people. You look up to so many people around you as your role models!

Ask yourself – how many of us have actually walked up to our role models and told them 'Sir / Madam, you are my role model. You have impacted my life and thoroughly inspired me to be a better person. I want to be like you.' How many? Honestly no one… right?

You may be tempted to say, 'I said that to my boss at our last party!' Sorry! Drunken confessions after four drinks are not considered true confessions of gratitude! Four drinks down, everyone loves everyone around and the world seems such a bright place. Or you may say, 'I said that to my girlfriend last week!' Rubbish! You had a fight with her and you didn't want to lose her. It was all made up; she is not your role model anyway! Or you may say, 'I sent a Thank You card to my teacher on the Teacher's Day!' Forget it! That card was designed by a designer unknown to you working in an unknown card printing company. You only picked it up because it looked nice. How would the designer know your feelings for your teacher?

We don't go and tell our role models that they are our role models because we think there is no need to! We think that the other person 'knows' it. Surprise! You can't be further from the truth.

Read this–

When Vijaya was felicitated by *Loksatta* (a leading Marathi daily) as 'NavDurga', the host of the ceremony asked her "Where did you get the strength to work till the last day of your pregnancy? Where did you get the courage to take your week-old baby to your meetings, training workshops and travel with her all the way?" Vijaya immediately replied "My maid, Pramila! It's her and people like her that tremendously inspire me. Because they have no choice, they work all the way through their pregnancy and are back at work before you even miss them! Pramila and thousands of women like her are my role models!"

This interview was published the next day on Loksatta's front page. Vijaya read it out to Pramila, who doesn't know how to read or write. There were tears in Pramila's eyes. She took a copy of the newspaper home and shared the article with all the women in her locality. One can only imagine the pride and joy she was experiencing.

It is not enough to have 'role models'. It is imperative to let them know, to tell them unequivocally that they ARE our role models. You might have said, 'I love you, Dad' a hundred times, but based on our experience of working with lakhs of people, we can with utmost surety say that you have not looked him the eye yet and told him that he is your role model.

By the same token, we can assume that there are several people who might be inspired by you, who might consider you their role model. These may be any one of your employees, subordinates, colleagues, bosses, vendors, customers. They may be your children, brothers, spouse, father and cousins. Every time they see you, they proudly announce 'There goes my brother/mother/boss/father/ wife.'

Did you know that Bhatia aunty next door always advises her son to be 'just like Raqshit Bhaiyya?' Rashmi maasi (aunt) always counsels her daughter to be 'just like Sapna didi (sister)'. That your son, when asked in class what he wants to be when he grows up, says proudly, 'I want to be just like my papa.' Or your daughter emulates your work ethic because she wants to achieve 'just like mummy.' She may even secretly dress in your clothes to be 'like mummy'.

Every grand decision of yours inspires them. Every success of yours motivates them. Every behavior of yours delights them. There are dozens if not hundreds who look up to you and take inspiration. You will never know it. But you are the hero to many out there who want to be 'just like you'.

> *You must have heard the story of the starfish a thousand times. For those who haven't, it is a parable of this small boy who is walking on the sea shore. Thousands of starfish are strewn on the sand brought in by the waves. A man, who is walking on the beach, watches the boy religiously pick up the starfish, one after after the other, and throws it back into the sea. "Son," the man tells the boy, "There are thousands of starfish on the sand. Your throwing back a few won't make much of a difference." Not looking up, the boy throws back one more into the sea and replies, "Made a difference to that one."*

You can be the boy or you can be the man. Make a difference or shrug your shoulders indifferently. But one thing is clear. Every right action by you is going to make a difference to someone somewhere, as is every wrong one.

You will never know it. But you are the hero to many who want to be just like you. And let that be your cross.

THE 5 BREAK FREE TRUTHS TRACKER – WEEK 6

Your Truth – I am too insignificant to make a difference.
The Truth – Each of us can make a significant difference.

What I Believed – 'My' Truth	*I am embarrassed to confess that I have not been too ethical in my business. I have insisted on doing only cash business with all my clients and have consciously avoided paying taxes. I have bribed so many people – government officials, policemen… always believing that 'the corrupt system' is too big for me to make a difference.*
What The Truth Is – My Realizations	*I realize that every unethical action of mine is being watched by the people whose respect I value – my wife, my subordinates, and especially my children. I realize that if I want the 'system' to change, I will have to change first. Because I am the system.*
My Next Step	*I will henceforth never bribe a policeman when I have broken a traffic signal. I will consciously make an effort to convert my 'all cash' business into 'white'. I will pay my taxes. I will appoint a business coach who is highly ethical to help me implement this in a phase wise manner. And I will not quote the swachchtaa abhiyaan to anyone unless I first clear up my act.*
My Truth Partner	*Prof. Amol Muley (Coach)*

THE 5 BREAK FREE TRUTHS TRACKER – WEEK 6

Your Truth – I am too insignificant to make a difference.
The Truth – Each of us can make a difference.

What I Believed – My Truth	
What The Truth Is – My Realizations	
My Next Step	
My Truth Partner	

For all of those who have read this book because you want to learn; and are curious to know what is stopping you from achieving the next level of success; and are constantly trying to discover yourselves –Congratulations! We are sure you have already found more than enough value in the pages that you have read.

Do write to us at vijaya@liberationcoaches.com and amol@liberationcoaches.com to let us know your experiences with The Truths. We will be more than happy to use your personal stories of success (with your names and your permission, of course) in our next book.

And finally, we want to thank you for enriching our life and the world with your presence and your experiences. Keep the blessings and wishes coming our way.

Here's wishing you an energizing, enabling and empowering life of liberation.

CASE STUDIES OF DISCOVERING 'THE' TRUTH

In this section, you will find several case studies of people with different beliefs each representing the Internal and External Loci of Control. This is how others have discovered The Truth using the Liberation Coaches' 4-Way Truth Test.

7

Case Studies of Discovering
The Truth

LIBERATION COACHES' 4-WAY TRUTH TEST FOR BELIEFS

Representing Internal Locus of Control

CASE STUDY 1

One of the participants attending Vijaya's *Mom to Supermom* workshop; a university-educated homemaker from a middle-class family shared her feeling thus – I won't ever be able to seek full-time employment... I will never be able to manage a job along with managing the household chores, my kids and my husband.

She had an extremely loving and supporting family. Her kids loved her, while her husband doted on her. She was well educated and her general knowledge was excellent. However, after marriage she hadn't stepped out of the home on her own nor taken up any assignment to keep herself busy. Now that the kids were becoming independent, she felt highly pressured to start doing something. Alas....she only *thought*, but *did* nothing.

Having applied the Liberation Coaches' 4-Way Truth Test to her belief, the results looked something like this –

Belief

I won't ever be able to seek full-time employment......I will never be able to manage a job along with managing the household chores, my kids and my husband.

4-Way Truth Test	Yes/ No	Outcome
1. Does My Truth reflect positively on me?	No (I haven't really given it a try yet!)	
2. Does My Truth reflect positively on others / circumstances?	No (Sounds like my husband and kids are not supportive at all.)	
3. Do I have any evidence to prove that my belief is The Truth?	No (Not really! There are dozens of my own friends from similar circumstances who are managing quite well)	My truth is far from The Truth
4. Does holding on to my truth make me feel empowered and in charge of the situation?	No (My belief has stopped me from even trying to apply for a job.)	

After intense personal coaching, the search for The Truth was finally successful. And the woman reached the following conclusion:

Sr. No.	My Truth	The Truth
1	I won't ever be able to seek full-time employment; I will never be able to manage a job along with managing the household chores, my kids and my husband.	I will talk to my kids and my husband about taking up a full-time job. They might support me. I might start with a part-time assignment to get a feel of the working environment and see how I can cope with all my household work and the job. I am sure everyone in the family will contribute to chores at home and it will not fall only on me.

Outcome: Today, after two years of working, she feels more fulfilled and independent. Her unavailability has made her children more independent and now she too has inspiring stories to share about how she overcomes her daily coordination challenges.

LIBERATION COACHES' 4-WAY TRUTH TEST

For Beliefs Representing Internal Locus of Control:

CASE STUDY 2

In another situation, a newly promoted factory manager shared something like this, "I don't think I'll be able to fulfil all the expectations of the top management. I haven't run a factory before." This guy was a star performer as the production manager and had amazing people skills, precisely the reasons why he was promoted.

The director of operations trusted him fully and was willing to mentor him on the way up the ladder. However, the promotion instead of motivating ended up terrifying him.

Having applied the Liberation Coaches 4-Way Truth Test to his belief, the results looked something like this–

Belief

I don't think I'll be able to fulfil all the expectations of the top management. I haven't run a factory before.

4-Way Test	Yes/ No	Outcome
1. Does My Truth reflect positively on me?	No (It shows me as an unsure and incompetent person)	My truth is far from The Truth
2. Does My Truth reflect positively on others/ circumstances?	No (It looks like I don't trust my management and my team!)	
3. Do I have any evidence to prove that my belief is The Truth?	No (Well….this is my first. I haven't done it before!)	
4. Does holding on to my truth make me feel empowered and in charge of the situation?	No (The thought has been giving me sleepless nights.)	

It took a lot of mentoring sessions and group coaching for the factory manager to realize the following Truth:

Sr. No.	My Truth	The Truth
2	I don't think I'll be able to fulfil all the expectations of the top management. I haven't run a factory before.	I must talk to the management and understand their expectations. I must identify all the areas that I need to learn in order to become an effective factory manager. I must make a self-development plan to improve in these areas.

Outcome: Today, after three years of working as an extremely successful factory manager, he is now being considered to head their largest overseas project.

LIBERATION COACHES 4-WAY TRUTH TEST

For Beliefs Representing External Locus of Control

CASE STUDY 3

One of our students, a steel trader from one of our advanced courses for entrepreneurship, believed that 'my industry is saturated and there are no further opportunities for growth'.

He had a committed team, an established clientele of over 20 years, an excellent range of products and a strong cash cushion to experiment with newer marketing strategies. However, when we met him first, all that he and his team were doing were repeating the same sales techniques and meeting the same clients over and over again.

This became a vicious circle. What was also happening was, whenever we would assemble the team for the reviews, they would come up with the same excuse, 'the market is saturated. Not our fault'.

Having applied the Liberation Coaches' 4-Way Test, the results looked something like this –

Belief:
My industry is saturated and there are no further opportunities for growth.

4-Way Test	Yes/ No	Outcome
1. Does My Truth reflect positively on me?	No (I sound very demotivated and like I have given up)	
2. Does My Truth reflect positively on others/ circumstances?	No (But well, you see… we are not getting enough orders!)	My truth is far from The Truth
3. Do I have any evidence to prove that my belief is The Truth?	No (Okay, there are a few traders who are growing but they are very few!)	
4. Does holding on to my truth make me feel empowered and in charge of the situation?	No (I'm not feeling empowered and in charge)	

On completion of the course, this amazing man discovered The Truth about his own beliefs and was a transformed man. This is how he realized The Truth:

Sr. No.	My Truth	The Truth
3	My industry is saturated and there are no further opportunities for growth.	I must study those few companies that have grown in these tough times and see for myself what their marketing strategies are. I must then talk to my team as to how we implement the same in our organization. Maybe if I changed my approach towards sales, I might get newer and larger orders.

Outcome: It has been three years since this discovery of 'The' Truth. Now there is no stopping him. He and his coach have recently reached the conclusion that he needs to adopt the strategy of Backward Integration, having won Dealer of the Year Award from his Principals. He is looking for a plot to set up his new factory.

LIBERATION COACHES 4-WAY TRUTH TEST

For Beliefs Representing External Locus of Control

CASE STUDY 4

In one of the organizations where we are empanelled to conduct year long training programs, a sales executive shared something like this – "I deserved this promotion owing to my performance last year. By not promoting me to the position of a sales manager, my organization hasn't played fairly with me."

This executive was young, had worked for two years with the organization after completing his MBA. His sales figures were outstanding and consistent over the two-year period. And of course, he earned far higher incentives than anyone in the sales team. However, he was found severely lacking in team work and leadership skills. He had conflicts with nearly everyone in his team and with several key players in other teams like accounts and production as well.

Having applied the Liberation Coaches' 4-Way Truth Test, the results looked something like this –

Belief

I deserved this promotion owing to my performance last year. By not promoting me to the position of a Sales Manager, my organization hasn't played fairly with me.

4-Way Test	Yes/ No	Outcome
1. Does My Truth reflect positively on me?	No (It kills me to tell others that I haven't been promoted!)	
2. Does My Truth reflect positively on others / circumstances?	No (They didn't promote me!)	My truth is far from The Truth
3. Do I have an evidence to prove that my belief is The Truth?	Yes (My performance… what more evidence do you want?)	
4. Does holding on to my truth makes me feel empowered and in charge of the situation?	No (If my performance won't satisfy them, then God knows what else will?!)	

Would you like to know what was closer to The Truth for this young talented sales professional which was programmed after several training programs and group mentoring sessions?

Sr. No.	My Truth	The Truth
4	I deserved this promotion owing to my performance last year. By not promoting me to the position of a sales manager, my organization hasn't played fairly with me.	May be there is something beyond mere sales performance in order to qualify for a sales manager's job. I must talk to my immediate boss and the HR Department to know more so that I can work upon developing those skill sets.

Outcome: It took one year of mentoring and four workshops to make him skilled in dealing with people, managing conflicts at work and having better working relationships with his team. He just got promoted finally to sales manager this year.

While outwardly it may seem easy to replace Their Truth with The Truth, in reality it is not.

All the four examples mentioned above are real and it took a lot of patience, training, counselling, cajoling, mentoring, probing and monitoring for us to get them to see The Truth. It was a painful journey for them as our students / trainees and it was equally a patience-testing journey for us as teachers / trainers to them.

The truth appears simple and evident when it pertains to someone else's life. But, the moment we are faced with the prospect of our dearly held beliefs being utter lies, the entire game changes! You must have seen for yourself in the book how difficult it can be to accept that Your Truth may not be The Truth after all.

But our experience over the years has shown that once you have shown the courage to reject our Truth, once you have accepted The Truth, life doesn't remain the same. Life changes... because You change! The world around you changes, people around you change, circumstances change, new opportunities open up... But all that will happen only once YOU change.

If you want to gain the most out of this book, follow this 'Truth Enabling Process'.

Truth Enabling Process

Our heartiest congratulations to you on picking up this book as you have taken the first step in identifying your beliefs and their relation with The Truth.

However, the steps that follow might be tough given how long you have been holding on to Your Truth. We wish you all the best for the journey of self-discovery, self-realization and self-transformation. Best of luck!

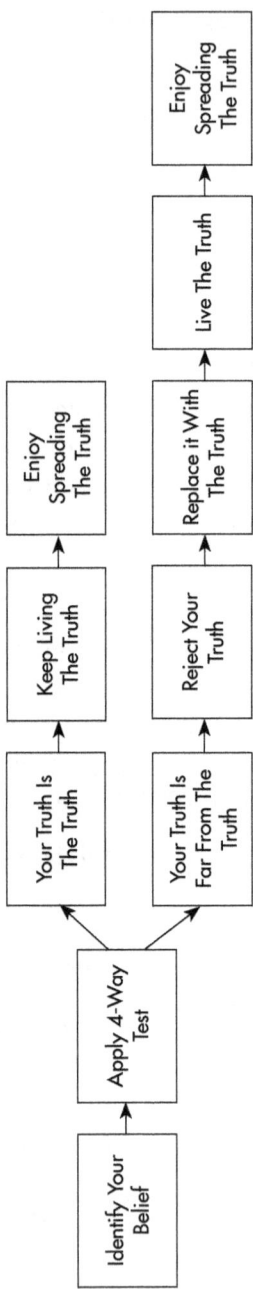

```
Identify Your
Belief
      │
      ▼
Apply 4-Way
   Test
   ┌──┴──┐
   ▼      ▼
Your Truth Is        Your Truth Is
The Truth            Far From The
   │                 Truth
   ▼                    │
Keep Living             ▼
The Truth          Reject Your
   │               Truth
   ▼                  │
Enjoy                 ▼
Spreading        Replace it With
The Truth        The Truth
                    │
                    ▼
                 Live The Truth
                    │
                    ▼
                 Enjoy
                 Spreading
                 The Truth
```

Acknowledgements

It is pretty much impossible to name all the people who have unconditionally contributed to our book, our business and our life. However, both of us are known for our *keeda* (zeal, in positive terms!) to try the impossible. Here we go!

Let us first, then, thank YOU, the reader. Where would authors be if they did not have generous, curious and inspiring patrons like you? Honestly, it takes a lot of courage and humility to pick up a book knowing that, in most cases, you already *know* what is written inside.

We want to thank our families, (The Suvarnas) Raqshit, Tapasya, Shalil (The Muleys) Indubai (grandmother and the pillar of strength), Vinod (Motthe Kaka), Vandana (Motthi Kaku), Ramakant (Bala Kaka), Varsha (Kaku), Vijay (Baba), Vaishali (Aai), Jayshree (Taai) and Anju (sister). Brothers and their amazingly loving wives – Prashant, Vaishali, Shyam, Smita, Aniruddha, Rajni, Mahesh, Archana, Vilas, Swati, Vidyadhar, Preeti, Manoj, Sheetal, Abhijit, Vijayta, Prathamesh, Nimish, Sumedh, Madhura, Mayuresh, Purva, Vineet, Ujjwal, Prajwal, Sai, Vijubhau (uncle), (The Iyers) V.S. Mani (Father, joy personified), Meenamani (Mother, pride personified), Venkatesh (Brother), (The Mudaliars) Varadarajan Thatha, Mariamma Paatti, Mohan Anna, Jayaram Anna, Bommi Akka, Jaani Anna, Gomati Akka, Indra Akka, Murthy Anna, Shyamala Anni.

A special thanks to the Ambekar family of Nagpur and the Suvarna family of Mumbai.

Our family, irrespective of the surnames they put, is not just a family; it's an institution in itself, one that taught us the values of love, camaraderie, self-respect and tolerance of all thoughts! Each person in our family is unique and so special that a separate book needs to be written on them. We are entirely a creation of their collected efforts. And are proud to say so! Mere 'thanks' are not enough.

Next in line are our friends – Ashish Babhulkar, Geeta Dipali, Abhijit Goho, Kanupriya Pandit, Surya Rao, Sita Sunil, , Abhijit Deshmukh, Sandeep Moon, Dr. Praful Gaikwad, Nandini Prashant, Rashi Bhadech, Bharatbhooshan Tiwari, Amit Sharma, Shirish Shahu, Vivek Joshi, Ashwin Gawande, Amit Kulkarni, Prashant Bansod, Sadique Khan, Sudhir Umberkar, Ajay Khobragade, Avinash Chavan, Shekhar Bharne, Krishnan Iyer, Gaurav Patil, Priya Sarnaik Patankar, Sugandha Jadhav, Madhura Shetty, J.C. Pande, Anil Warkad, Teresa Borges, Amit Rao, Pankaj Sonawane, Ranjit Singh Khehra, Ashish Patil, Pulin Mehta, Sunita Suresh, Sujata Swamy, Nandini Shridhar and Anjali Achan.

Our friends are the source of our strength. They've always made us aware of the fallacies and the stupidities we're capable of. They are the ones who keep us grounded. Thanks fellows! (Most of you have promised to 'buy' the book and not ask for a free copy. Now that's the ultimate sacrifice.)

Thanks to Our Ex-Colleagues who made Liberation Coaches what it is today – Saroj Dayal, Nilesh Namase, Nilesh Misal, Suchi Pabari, Rana Mukherjee, Reema Parsurampuria, Yogesh, Vijayata, Rohit Ahuja, Kiran Murkar, Manju Nair, Poonam Dhanani, Suman Vyas, Babita Patel, Vishal Pandya and Tulshiram Potkule.

And Team Liberation Coaches – Venkatesh Subramaniam, Priya Dhingra, Sanket Sawant (who worked day and night to typeset this book), Sandesh Mogare, Rasik Sankpal.

We were able to take out time to write this book, only because you were managing the business activities, the performance reviews at our clients' organizations, training workshops all across

India, the consultancy and coaching projects and of course the payments (most importantly the inward ones). Thank you.

We also want to thank the Liberation Coaches – Extended Family – Consultants & Business Associates – Mr. B.K. Pansari, Mr. Sadashiv Borgaonkar, Mr. Sriram Iyer, Mrs. Kavita Hans, Mrs. Sujata Prabhu, Mr. Yogeshwar Vashishtha, Mr. Mohnish Nair, Prof. Jeet Shah, Adv. Devendra Singh and several others.

On our own, we would have been a 'two-man-partnership', nothing more than that. Today, Liberation Coaches is empowering 500 companies across the nation, only because of you. Thank you.

Our Accounting Team – Alpesh Dangodra (our accountant), Mr. Nilesh Lakhani (our auditor and CA), Parag Shah (CA- service tax consultant)

Our Teachers – Mrs. Deshpande, Mrs. Wakare, Anil Titre sir, Dr. Vijay Singh Dahima, Dr. Seema Mahajan, Dr. Vidya Naik, Nancy Teacher, Ustaad Mehboob Khan, Mr. Rajneesh Bisht, Prof. Venkat Subramaniam… and the list goes on.

You believed in us. That was enough to lead two ordinary minds on the quest to success.

A BIG thank you to our Mentors –

Mr. Sushil Dange, Mr. Bhavin Gandhi, Mrs. Micky Bhatia, Mr. Ronnie Screwvala, Mr. Santosh Nair (you taught us the 'T' of training, Sir), Mrs. Anuradha Shankar (IG – MP Police), Prof. V.B. Joshi, Prof. Hafeez Iqbal, Mr. Pramod Gothi (we are truly honoured to be coached by you, Sir), Dr. Ashok Khanvte, Mr. Rajesh Tagore (this book wouldn't have come out at least for another ten years, had you not been there!), Mr. Vineet Kapoor (AIG – MP Police) and Mr. Deepak Dhabalia (Mentor, Client, Friend, Well-Wisher)

Everything that we think, do or say is what we have picked up from our Mentors. If there's anything worth learning from us, it has been planted by you. Thank you.

And Lastly our Clients – Mr. Sai Chandar (Mahindra & Mahindra), Mr. Anil Seth and Mr. Gaurav Malhotra (Nestle India Ltd.), Mr. Oscar Noronha (Transocean), Mr. Romesh Kaul (Mahindra Gears), Mr. Deepak Chhibba (MIQ), Mr. Girish Kothari, Vitthal Bhai Patel, Manibhai Patel, the Dedhias – Jagdishbhai, Sanjaybhai, Manishbhai, Mr. Jignesh Dhabalia, Mr. Saurabh Shah, Rajulbhai Shah, Hiteshbhai & Darshanbhai Mevada, Mr. Nikhil Naik, Pradeepbhai Parikh, Lalitbhai Pandya, Naineshbhai Pandya, Mr. Hiten Shah, Mrs. Avani Shah, Mrs. Manisha Sangani, the Jalans – Shri S.M., Rajeshji, Dineshji, Riteshji, the Seksarias – Brij, Raj and Chander, Vipul Kedia, the Malviyas – Sonaramji, Shankarji, Karan, the Mevadas – Dilipbhai, Raj, Jigar, the Patels – Kamleshbhai and Mukeshbhai, Mr. Apurva Shah, Mr. Rajiv Parikh, the Jadhavs – Bipinji and Nitinji, Mr. Kishor Naik, Mr. Arun Shinde, Mrs. Hema Bhatwadekar, Mr. Sashis Lohidaksh, Mr. Manoj Gada, the Minochas – Manishji, Hemantji, Sumitji, the Devnanis – Sunilji and Anilji, the Rathis – Ganeshji, Kishor and Varun, the Mirchandanis – Vijayji, Kishoreji and Aditya, the Shahs – Nikhil and Chirag, Mr. Milan Shah, Mr. Tulshidas Sawant and hundreds of others. You, only YOU have made us 'Trainers, Consultants and Coaches'. In spite of being amazingly successful yourselves, you have given us the opportunity to touch your lives meaningfully and to contribute to your organizations. We have learnt far more from our associations with you than through turning pages of a hundred books. And we still do!

Our Students, Participants of Our Training Workshops and Seminars – Your number is in lakhs, hence difficult to mention. Yet, all of you have consciously and unconsciously contributed your dialogues, stories and life experiences, glimpses of which you will see in this book. Please don't ask for royalty. Instead show us the paragraph which is your story or dialogue or experience and we will give you a discount during our next workshop!

And lastly, we want to thank each other.

Vijaya – Amol has brought out the best in me. He has changed my paradigms about so many things that I am a better human being now. He has opened my mind to ideas and possibilities that I could never have thought about for myself. He has accepted me into his family seamlessly and I feel blessed with all the love that the Muleys shower upon me all the time. If I am competitive, then let me confess, he is my fiercest competitor, and for me that is the ultimate compliment. His understanding and patience are formidable. His relationship building skills are extraordinary. His complete acceptance & loyalty are inspiring. He has made me comfortable with myself and he is my strongest advocate. Liberation Coaches was conceived by him and I want to thank him for inviting me to be a part of it. And lastly, he plays the role of mentor, coach, competitor, co-director, teammate, colleague, punch-bag and best friend. And that about says it all. Thank you, Amol!

Amol – Vijaya is my best friend and it's an honour calling her one. She has earned it in every respect. I'm yet to come across someone as talented, as competent and as committed as her. When she takes up a task, one can be rest assured that the best, and only the best will be delivered. She's played a dozen roles around me. I can think of no other parallel that can come even remotely close to her enthusiasm and commitment – a colleague, a fierce competitor (yes, both of us were competing fiercely for the CEO's position in the last organization we worked for!), a devoted co-director, a co-trainer and now a co-author. But, the one role she has truly set a benchmark in is the role of being my best friend. My best friend has encouraged me, motivated me, criticised me and at times challenged me… to make me better! And people who know me will vouch for the fact that her presence in my life for the past ten years has made me a better man, every day. Thank you Vijaya!

About the Authors

About Vijaya

Vijaya is a Mumbai University Topper in MHRDM and started her formal career in 1993. She had always wanted to join the IPS, but couldn't fulfil her dream. And today she is a Master Trainer with the Indian Police Department. She is a maverick with diverse interests, expertise and accomplishments. From human psychology & organizational processes to music, painting, dancing and writing, from maths puzzles and logical analysis to people management and module creation, she has numerous awards to her credit. She is a pioneer of the Mom to SuperMom Movement and likes working with youth. She enjoys solitude but you will never know it if you meet her. She is passionate and intense and believes in old-fashioned concepts like hard work and ethics. She loves challenges, aspires to work till she dies at the age of 110 and is always ready to defend what is right, much to the amusement and despair of her kids, Raqshit and Tapasya. She loves Mumbai, the city which enabled her to achieve so much. From extremely humble beginnings to being a role model to lakhs of people, Vijaya considers herself truly blessed and is the first to agree that her life is too exciting and wonderful to be true.

About Amol

Amol hails from the quaint town of Wardha and is an MBA in HR from Mumbai University. He was born for the stage and continually lives his dream of performing in front of an audience.

His grasp over the usage of Hindi and Marathi to connect with the audience is formidable. He enjoys being with people and people enjoy being with him. His sense of humour is amazing and he can keep you in splits for hours. His expertise and successes are in the field of Sales, Marketing and Organizational Strategies. He is an accomplished tabla player and loves Indian Classical Music. He is a true connoisseur of performing arts. He has won several awards for training and is considered one of the top motivational speakers in the country. He loves adventure activities and hates ghost movies. He intends to die partying when he is 110. He is the first person his friends call if they are in trouble and he is ever ready to offer motivation, advice, money and his own home if need be. He will do things because they are exciting and will find excitement if they are not. He is easy going, cheerful and takes immense pleasure in his super-extended family.

About Liberation Group

The Vision of the Group is to
Energize, Enable and Empower
People to Live a Liberated Life.

Vijaya and Amol are the Founder Directors and Liberation Group itself has a panel of more than a hundred faculty, associates, principal consultants and trainers.

Liberation Coaches is a multiple National and International Award winning organization that is in the business of Organization Development, Organization Transformation through Training, Business Coaching and Consultancy. It has its presence in cities all across India and also has affiliates in Thailand, Singapore and Malaysia. LCPL is known for its high energy training workshops, implementation oriented business solutions and delegation focused business coaching initiatives.

Liberation Education Trust works with the government, NGOs, schools and women and children on parallel education. Mom to SuperMom and Genext are not just programs, but Empowerment Movements for Women and Children, while the Learning and Education Tools are developed by Liberation Learning Systems.

Visit www.liberationcoaches.com for more details.

www.ingramcontent.com/pod-product-compliance
Lightning Source LLC
Chambersburg PA
CBHW022123080426
42734CB00006B/233